AMONG FRIENDS

Is it Soup Yet?

A Cookbook for Soup Lovers

RECIPES BY DOT VARTAN
ILLUSTRATIONS BY SHELLY REEVES SMITH

**Andrews McMeel
Publishing**

Kansas City

ACKNOWLEDGMENTS

Special thanks to my family and friends, especially my husband Gentre,
my sister Stephanie, and my friend Michelle.

99 00 01 02 RDC 10 9 8 7 6 5 4 3 2

LIBRARY OF CONGRESS CATALOGING-IN-PUBLICATION DATA
Vartan, Dot.
Is is soup yet? : recipes / by Dot Vartan ; illustrated by Shelly Reeves Smith.
p.   cm.
ISBN: 0-8362-6993-4
1. Soups. I. Title
TX757.V37 1998
641.8'13—dc21   98-7477
CIP

ATTENTION: SCHOOLS AND BUSINESSES

Andrews McMeel books are available at quantity discounts with bulk purchase for educational, business, or sales promotional use. For information, please write to: Special Sales Department, Andrews McMeel Publishing, 4520 Main Street, Kansas City, Missouri 64111.

I love soup!

There's nothing more satisfying than a hearty bowl of soup for lunch or dinner. Of course, you can't have soup without some type of bread to accompany it. In my case, muffins. And muffins were what brought me to create this soup cookbook.

After writing a muffin cookbook and eating meals of muffin samples, I decided that I needed to round out the menu with something more hearty. Soup was the perfect choice. There can be no better meal than a delicious soup served with a scrumptious muffin.

So I began my soup cookbook by compiling a list of my favorite soups. Then I gathered up my stock pots and began cooking. While I cooked, I made many new discoveries. I discovered new vegetables— like rutabaga, fennel bulbs, horseradish and okra. I can even identify them in the vegetable market now! I discovered how to make chicken broth—it's easy! I discovered that there are many types of canned tomatoes on the grocery store shelf. I'll bet I tried every one of them, too. Best of all, I discovered that making soup is easy and fun.

The nice thing about cooking soup is that once you're done preparing it, you put it on the stove and do not have to worry about it for an hour or so. Crock pot soups are even better. In the morning, you put all of the ingredients into the pot, go to work and when you arrive home you are greeted with a delicious aroma and even better, dinner is ready!

Don't have all day to cook soup? Don't worry. Many of my recipes take less than one hour and some only take 20 minutes. To help you gauge the time, I've indicated an approximate cooking time for each recipe.

Now it's your turn to discover how easy and fun making soup can be. I hope you enjoy cooking my favorite soup recipes. Don't be afraid to add a little of this and a little of that to accommodate your tastes, and remember, a good soup meal is not complete without fresh bread or muffins.

Enjoy!

TABLE OF
CONTENTS

HEARTY BEANS & CROCK COOKERY   49

MAIN DISH SOUPS   65

Chicken

A CHICKEN IN EVERY POT

YANKEE DOODLE NOODLE COMPANY

PAPRIKA   PEPPER   SALT

Chicken Noodle

SRS

Chicken Noodle

Yield: 8 servings
Cooking time: 2 hours

3 lb. fryer
3 bay leaves
6 peppercorns
7 stalks of celery
2 cups chicken broth
1 large onion, minced
3 carrots, julienne sliced

1 tablespoon dried parsley
1/2 lb. thin egg noodles
1 (10 oz.) package frozen peas
3 teaspoons salt
1 teaspoon ground white pepper
1/2 teaspoon Accent™ seasoning

Remove the neck and gizzard pack from the cavity of the chicken. Place the chicken into a 6 quart stock pot and cover with water. Add the bay leaves, peppercorns and 3 stalks celery, broken in half. Cook over high heat until the water comes to a boil. Reduce the heat and simmer for 1 hour or until the chicken falls off the bone. Remove the chicken to cool and strain the broth. Return the liquid to the stock pot. Add 2 cups chicken broth, minced onion, 4 stalks minced celery, carrots, dried parsley, and egg noodles. Cook over high heat until the noodles are soft. Chop the chicken into bite size pieces and add with the peas to the broth. Season with salt, white pepper, and Accent™. Cook for approximately 10 minutes or until the peas are heated through.

I made this for the first time when my husband was ill. It was the perfect cure for him. And once I learned how easy it was to cook the chicken to make the broth, I will always make broth this way.

Chicken Corn Chowder

Yield: 8 servings
Cooking time: 2 hours

3 lb. fryer, approx.
3 bay leaves
6 peppercorns
6 stalks of celery
1/3 cup minced onion
1/3 cup minced green pepper
6 ears of corn, shucked and cut off cob

1/8 teaspoon garlic powder
4 teaspoons salt
1 teaspoon ground white pepper
1 1/4 cups skim milk
1 cup flour

Remove the neck and gizzard pack from the cavity of the chicken. Place the chicken into a 6 quart stock pot and cover with water. Add the bay leaves, peppercorns and 3 stalks celery, broken in half. Cook over high heat until the water comes to a boil. Reduce the heat and simmer for 1 hour or until the chicken falls off the bone. Remove the chicken to cool and strain the broth. Return the liquid to the stock pot. Add 3 stalks minced celery, minced onion, green pepper, corn, garlic powder, salt and pepper. Cook over medium heat for 15 minutes.
Chop the chicken into bite size pieces and add to the broth. In a small bowl, whisk together the skim milk and the flour. Add to the soup to thicken. Heat through and serve.

This thick, rich chicken soup will warm you up on a cold, fall evening.

Chicken Cilantro Bisque

Yield: 8 servings
Cooking time: 30 minutes

1 lb. boneless skinless chicken breasts
  (4 breasts), cut into chunks
4 cups chicken broth
1 cup fresh cilantro leaves, chopped
1/3 cup minced onion
1/2 cup minced celery

1 minced garlic clove
1/2 teaspoon ground cumin
1 teaspoon salt
1/4 teaspoon ground white pepper
1/3 cup flour
1 cup half and half

In a 4 quart stock pot, combine the chicken, broth, cilantro leaves, onion, celery, garlic, cumin, salt, and pepper. Bring to a boil. Reduce heat to low and simmer, covered, for 20 minutes, until the chicken is tender. Pour into a food processor and add flour. Purée until smooth. Pour back into stock pot. Cook over medium heat until soup comes to a boil. Turn heat to low. Stir in half and half and heat through. Be careful not to scald the soup. Serve.

Parsley   Thyme   Cilantro

Calico Chicken

Yield: 6 servings
Cooking time: 45 minutes

3 tablespoons olive oil
1 cup onion, minced
2 celery stalks, minced
2 garlic cloves, minced
1 lb. boneless chicken breasts,
    skinned and cubed
1 (14.5 oz.) can diced tomatoes
1/2 cup carrots, diced
6 cups chicken stock

1/2 teaspoon ground thyme
1/8 teaspoon ground white pepper
1 teaspoon salt
1/2 lb. green beans, cut into 1 inch
    pieces
1/2 cup fresh corn
1 cup zucchini, diced
1 small red pepper, minced
2 tablespoons finely chopped parsley

In a 4 quart stock pot, heat the olive oil. Add the onion and celery and sauté for 5 minutes on medium heat. Add the garlic and chicken and sauté, stirring often, for 10 minutes. Add the tomatoes, carrots, chicken stock, ground thyme, white pepper and salt. Bring to a boil, lower heat, cover and simmer for 20 minutes. Add the green beans, corn, zucchini, red pepper. Cover and cook for 10 minutes. Stir in the parsley. Serve.

 Fresh, colorful vegetables give this chicken soup a wonderful flavor and a festive look.

Chicken with Gouda Cheese

Yield: 8 servings
Cooking time: 40 minutes

3 tablespoons olive oil
1 large onion, chopped
1 garlic clove, minced
1 tablespoon ground coriander
1 1/2 teaspoons caraway seeds
8 cups chicken broth
2 cups butternut squash, peeled and
  diced

1 1/2 lbs. boneless, skinless,
  chicken breasts, cut into 1/2 inch
  cubes
1 (15 oz.) can light red kidney
  beans
2 teaspoons salt
1/4 teaspoon ground white pepper
7 oz. Gouda cheese, shredded

   Heat the olive oil in a 6 quart stock pot. Add the onion, garlic, ground coriander, and caraway seeds, and sauté for 10 minutes. Add the chicken broth and squash. Bring to a boil, lower heat, cover and simmer for 10 minutes. Add the cubed chicken, salt and pepper. Cover and simmer for 20 minutes. Add the kidney beans and heat through. Stir in the shredded Gouda cheese and serve.

   The caraway seeds blended with the Gouda cheese create wonderful flavors in this chicken soup recipe.

Chicken with Dumplings

Yield: 8 servings
Cooking time: 60 minutes

1/3 cup all-purpose flour
1 teaspoon salt
1/2 teaspoon freshly ground pepper
2 tablespoons vegetable oil
3 lb. quartered fryer
3 small onions, quartered
2 cloves garlic, minced
8 cups chicken broth
4 carrots, sliced

2 stalks of celery, sliced
1 medium sized turnip, peeled and
   diced
4 small red potatoes, diced
1/4 teaspoon thyme
1 (10 oz.) package frozen peas

Dumplings
1 cup all-purpose flour
2 teaspoons baking powder
1/4 teaspoon salt
Dash of freshly ground pepper
2 tablespoons vegetable shortening
1/2 cup milk

Combine the flour, 1/2 teaspoon salt and pepper in a large plastic self-sealing bag. Pat chicken dry and place it, one piece at a time, in the bag. Seal bag and shake well to coat the chicken. Remove the chicken, shake off the excess flour and set aside.

In a 4 quart stock pot, heat the oil over medium-high heat. Add two pieces of the chicken and cook until golden, about 4 minutes per side. Set aside and cook the other pieces. Discard all but 2 tablespoons of the drippings.

Cook the onions and garlic in the drippings for 5 minutes. Add the chicken broth, carrots, celery, turnip, red potatoes, 1/2 teaspoon salt and thyme. Bring to a boil, reduce heat, cover and simmer for 30 minutes. Remove the chicken, and skin it, being careful not to burn yourself. Cut the meat from the bones. Return the meat to the stock pot. Stir in the peas and turn the heat to medium high.

To make the dumplings, combine the flour, baking powder, salt and pepper in a medium-sized bowl. With a pastry blender, cut in shortening until mixture resembles coarse crumbs. Stir in the milk, just until combined. Drop batter by heaping tablespoons into the soup. You should have approximately 10 dumplings. Cover and simmer for 10 minutes. Serve.

Everyone will love this down-home thick, rich soup!

Chicken Gumbo

Yield: 4 servings
Cooking time: 45 minutes

2 tablespoons olive oil
1 medium onion, minced
2 stalks celery, sliced
1 garlic clove, minced
1 small green pepper, chopped
1 whole boneless, skinless chicken
  breast, cubed
1 cup okra, sliced
1 (28 oz.) can crushed tomatoes
1 cup chicken stock
1 teaspoon dried oregano
1 teaspoon ground thyme
1/2 teaspoon salt
1/2 teaspoon hot sauce

In a 4 quart stock pot, heat the olive oil over medium high heat. Add the onion and celery and sauté for 5 minutes on medium heat. Add the garlic, green pepper, and chicken and sauté, stirring often, for 10 minutes. Add the okra, crushed tomatoes, chicken stock, oregano, thyme, salt and hot sauce. Stir well. Bring to a boil, lower heat, cover and simmer for 30 minutes. Serve as a thick soup or over cooked rice.

During cooking, the texture of okra goes through several stages. It must be cooked long enough to be tender-crisp.

Chicken Matzoball

Yield: 8 servings
Cooking time: 45 minutes

2 tablespoons vegetable oil
2 large eggs
1/2 cup matzo meal

1 teaspoon salt
2 tablespoons chicken broth
8 cups chicken broth, preferably homemade

In a mixing bowl, beat together the oil and eggs. Mix in the matzo meal, salt and 2 tablespoons chicken broth. Cover and refrigerate for 15 minutes. Pour the 8 cups chicken broth into a 4 quart stock pot and bring to a boil. Lower heat slightly and reduce to a gentle boil. Form the matzo dough into 1inch balls. The dough should make 8 balls that once cooked will expand to 3 inch size. Drop the balls into the lightly boiling broth. Cover and cook for 30 minutes. Do not lift the lid while cooking. Serve.

Matzoballs are a very light dumpling. Served traditionally in plain chicken broth, you can enhance the broth by adding your favorite chopped vegetables.

Chicken and Ham Pot Pie

Yield: 8 servings
Cooking time: 60 minutes

5 cups chicken broth
1 large fennel bulb, chopped
2 lbs. boneless, skinless chicken
   breasts, diced
1 cup carrots, diced
1/2 cup celery, diced
1/4 cup onion, diced
1 cup frozen peas
2 teaspoons fennel seeds
1/2 teaspoon salt
5 tablespoons unsalted butter
5 tablespoons flour

2 1/2 cups milk (not lowfat)
2 tablespoons lemon juice
1/4 lb. thinly sliced smoked ham, cut
   into match-stick strips

Pie Crust:
3 cups sifted all purpose flour
3/4 teaspoon salt
3/4 cup chilled, unsalted butter, cut
   into pieces
4 1/2 tablespoons chilled shortening
6 tablespoons ice water

Bring the chicken broth to a boil in a 4 quart stock pot. Add the chopped fennel and cook over medium-high heat for 5 minutes. Add the chicken, carrots, peas, celery, onion, salt and fennel seed. Simmer over medium heat until the chicken is cooked through, about 10 minutes.

In the meantime, melt the butter in a medium-size saucepan. Gradually stir in the flour and then the milk, whisking until smooth. Stir in the lemon juice. Add to the soup with the ham strips and simmer until all ingredients are blended, about 10 minutes. (You may serve the soup at this point without the pie crust topping.) Ladle the soup into 8 ovenproof soup bowls and make the pie crust topping.

Preheat oven to 375°. In a large bowl, sift together the flour and salt. With a pastry blender, cut in the butter and then the shortening. Add 4 tablespoons of the chilled water and blend in with a fork. Add enough additional water by tablespoons until a moist dough is formed. Gather dough into a ball and place on a floured surface. Roll out the dough to 1/8 inch thickness. Cut out 8 rounds, each measuring 1/2 to 1 inch larger in diameter than your soup bowls. Gather and reroll the dough as necessary. Lay 1 dough round over each dish. Press dough overhang firmly to adhere to sides and top rim of dish. Cut slits in the dough for steam to escape. Place pies on a large baking sheet. Bake until crusts are golden brown, about 30 minutes. Serve.

The traditional chicken pot pie takes on a new look and taste with the addition of ham and served as a soup.

Chicken Passatelli

Yield: 8 servings
Cooking time: 35 minutes

8 cups chicken broth
2 large carrots, chopped
1 stalk celery, chopped
2 garlic cloves, minced
1/2 teaspoon salt
1/4 teaspoon ground oregano
1 whole skinless, boneless chicken
   breast, diced

1 1/2 cups fresh Italian bread crumbs
2/3 cups grated Parmesan cheese
1 teaspoon nutmeg
2 eggs
1 cup chopped fresh parsley

   Bring the chicken broth to a boil in a 4 quart stock pot. Add the carrots, celery, garlic, salt, oregano and chicken. Reduce heat to medium-low and simmer for 30 minutes. In a small bowl, combine the bread crumbs, cheese and nutmeg. Beat the eggs in a separate bowl. Add to the bread crumbs and mix to form a dough. Add a little water if the dough is too dry, or a few more bread crumbs if too moist. To form the passatelli, roll the dough between your palms into a rope about 1/4 inch thick. Break into 1/2 inch lengths. Form the rest of the dough this way. Bring the broth back to a boil. Add the passatelli and parsley and cook for 5 minutes. Serve sprinkled with a little Parmesan cheese.

The Italian version of chicken and dumplings. Delicious!

Creamless Cream of Chicken

Yield: 8 servings
Cooking time: 50 minutes

9 cups chicken broth
1 small onion, chopped
1 bay leaf
1 1/2 cups white rice
1 (13.75 oz.) can beef broth
1 cup sliced leeks
1 cup sliced carrots
1 cup sliced celery
1 teaspoon salt
1/2 teaspoon ground white pepper

2 cups cooked, shredded chicken
1/2 cup dry white wine
Fresh parsley garnish

Pour 4 cups of the chicken stock into a 4 quart stock pot. Reserve the other 5 cups. Add the rice, bay leaf and onion. Bring to a boil, cover and simmer for 20 minutes. Remove the bay leaf. Purée the soup in batches in a blender, being careful not to splatter the hot liquid. Add some of the reserved chicken broth to the blender to thin the purée. Return the purée to the stock pot. Add the remaining chicken stock and the beef broth. Add the vegetables, salt and pepper. Cook over medium-high heat for 20 minutes, or until the vegetables are soft. Add the chicken and wine and simmer for 10 minutes. Serve sprinkled with chopped parsley.

You'll enjoy this thick cream of chicken soup because it tastes so good and because it is low in fat--no cream!

Chicken with Rice

Yield: 8 servings
Cooking time: 1 hour 45 minutes

1 3 lb. fryer
3 bay leaves
6 peppercorns
5 stalks celery
10 cups water
1 medium onion, minced
4 teaspoons salt
1 tablespoon butter
1/4 cup fine dried egg noodles
1 cup long grain rice
1/2 teaspoon ground white pepper
1 tablespoon parsley flakes

Remove the neck and gizzard pack from the cavity of the chicken.
Place the chicken into a 6 quart stock pot and cover with 10 cups water.
Add the bay leaves, peppercorns and 3 stalks of celery, broken in half.
  Cook over high heat until the water comes to a boil. Reduce heat and
simmer for 1 hour or until the chicken falls off the bone. Remove the
chicken to cool and strain the broth. Return the liquid to the stock pot.
Mince the remaining 2 stalks of celery and the onion. Add to the chicken

stock with the salt and bring to a boil. Melt the butter in a small frying pan or saucepan. Add the dried egg noodles and sauté for 5 minutes over medium-high heat until brown. Add the rice and sauté for 5 minutes more. Pour into the boiling chicken stock. Reduce heat, cover and simmer for 30 minutes. In the meantime, remove the meat from the chicken.

Chop the white meat into bite-sized pieces. Set aside the dark meat. (Use it for another recipe. See page 124.) Add the chicken, white pepper and parsley flakes. Stir well and cook for 5 minutes until the chicken is heated through.

This recipe combines my mother-in-law's rice pilaf with chicken soup. Wonderful!

Grilled Chicken with Artichoke

Yield: 8 servings
Cooking time: 1 hour 20 minutes

1 oz. dried porcini mushrooms
2 whole skinless, boneless chicken
  breasts, halved
1/4 cup olive oil
1 medium red onion, minced
3 garlic cloves, minced
1/4 teaspoon freshly ground black
  pepper
1/2 cup finely chopped fresh parsley
2 (14 oz.) cans artichoke hearts,
  drained and chopped
6 cups chicken broth

1 1/2 oz. sun-dried tomatoes (not
  packed in oil), snipped into
  small pieces
2 tablespoons lemon juice
2 tablespoons tomato paste
1/2 cup dry white wine
Parmesan cheese garnish

In a small bowl, cover the dried mushrooms with 1 cup of very hot water. Let stand until softened, about 20 minutes.

Season the chicken breasts with salt and pepper. On a grill or under the broiler, cook the chicken breasts for 15 minutes or until done. Set aside. Drain the mushrooms, saving the soaking liquid. Finely chop the mushrooms.

In a large skillet, heat the olive oil. Add the mushrooms, onion, garlic, pepper, and parsley. Cook over medium-high heat for 5 minutes, stirring often. Add the chopped artichokes and cook for 10 minutes. In the meantime, pour the chicken broth into a 6 quart stock pot. Bring to a boil. Add the sun-dried tomatoes. Lower heat and simmer for 15 minutes.

In a small bowl, whisk together the reserved mushroom soaking liquid, lemon juice, tomato paste, and white wine. Stir into the chicken broth. Add the cooked vegetables and mix well. Cut the chicken breasts lengthwise into strips. Add to the soup. Heat through and serve with a Parmesan cheese garnish.

The combination of mushrooms, artichokes and sun-dried tomatoes creates a very exotic chicken soup.

Oriental Chicken

Yield: 6 servings
Cooking time: 30 minutes

8 cups chicken broth
1 boneless, skinless whole chicken
    breast, diced
Juice of 1 lemon
1 large carrot, julienne sliced
6 scallions, finely sliced

1 cup pea pods, sliced diagonally in
    half
1 cup chopped fresh spinach
2 teaspoons salt
1/2 teaspoon white pepper
1 tablespoon grated gingerroot

Pour the chicken broth into a 6 quart stock pot and bring to a boil. Add the diced chicken, fresh lemon juice and carrots. Cook over medium heat for 15 minutes. Add the scallions, pea pods, chopped spinach, salt, pepper and gingerroot. Cook for 15 more minutes. Serve.

In the tradition of oriental soups, this is a light chicken soup with an accent of ginger.

Vegetable

Artichoke

Yield: 6 servings
Cooking time: 40 minutes

1 tablespoon olive oil
1 leek, white part only, sliced
1 large potato, peeled and diced
1 celery stalk, chopped
4 cups beef broth

1/2 teaspoon thyme
2 (14 oz.) cans artichoke hearts, drained and chopped
1 tablespoon lemon juice
Parmesan cheese

In a 4 quart stock pot, sauté the leeks, potatoes, and celery in the oil over high heat for 5 minutes. Add the beef broth, thyme and artichoke hearts and bring to a boil. Reduce heat, cover and simmer until potatoes are tender, about 30 minutes. In a food processor, purée the soup in batches, being careful not to splatter the hot liquid. Return the purée to the stock pot. Stir in the lemon juice. Heat through and serve sprinkled with Parmesan cheese.

When you have a taste for artichokes, make this recipe. Serve this as a first course to your meal and your guests will rave over your exotic cooking!

Black Olive Potato

Yield: 6 servings
Cooking time: 30 minutes

2 medium-sized potatoes, peeled
    and diced
1 cup chicken broth
1 (7 oz.) can sliced, ripe olives,
    drained

2 (8 oz.) bottles clam juice
1/4 teaspoon freshly ground black
    pepper
1 tablespoon grated lemon rind
1/3 cup sour cream

Place the potatoes and chicken broth into a large saucepan. Bring to a boil, lower heat, cover and simmer for 20 minutes. Add the drained olives and clam juice. Bring to a boil, reduce heat and simmer for 5 minutes. In a food processor, purée the soup in batches, being careful not to splatter the hot liquid. Return the purée to the saucepan. Stir in the black pepper and grated lemon rind. Heat through. Serve topped with a dollop of sour cream.

Olives aren't just for garnishing with this soup. Serve it as a first course for your Italian or Greek feast.

Brussels Sprout Bisque

Yield: 6 servings
Cooking time: 45 minutes

4 tablespoons butter
1 onion, chopped
1 potato, chopped
4 cups washed, trimmed,
    quartered brussels sprouts
3 1/2 cups chicken broth
1/2 cup dry white wine
1 tablespoon white wine
    Worcestershire sauce
1/4 teaspoon mace
1/2 teaspoon salt
1/8 teaspoon ground white
    pepper
2 bay leaves
1 1/2 tablespoons flour
1 cup half and half
1/8 teaspoon nutmeg

In a 4 quart stock pot, melt the butter. Add the onion and potato and sauté for 5 minutes. Add the brussels sprouts and cook for another 5 minutes, stirring constantly. Add the chicken broth, wine, Worcestershire sauce, mace, salt, and pepper. Bring to a boil, stirring constantly. Reduce the heat and add the bay leaves. Cover and simmer for 20 minutes until the brussels sprouts are tender, but not overcooked. Remove the bay leaves. Pour the soup in batches into the food processor. Blend until smooth, being careful not to splatter the hot liquid. Pour back into the stock pot. Turn heat to low. Place the flour into a small bowl. Add 1 tablespoon of the half and half and stir to make a paste. Stir into the soup. Add the remaining half and half and nutmeg. Stir until heated through. Serve.

🍃 This is a new and delicious way to serve brussels sprouts.

Cabbage

Yield: 6 servings
Cooking time: 1 hour 5 minutes

1 1/2 tablespoons vegetable oil
1 medium-sized onion, chopped
2 stalks celery, chopped
1/2 cup white wine
1 (32 oz.) jar V-8™ juice

1 (8 oz.) can tomato sauce
1 chicken bouillon cube
1 teaspoon garlic powder
1 head cabbage, shredded

In a 4 quart stock pot, sauté the onion and celery in the oil for 5 minutes. Stir in the white wine, V-8™ juice, tomato sauce, chicken bouillon cube and garlic powder. Bring to a boil. Stir in the shredded cabbage, reduce heat and simmer, covered, for 1 hour.

The V-8™ juice spices up the cabbage in this easy recipe.

Celery

Yield: 4 servings
Cooking time: 60 minutes

6 tablespoons butter
2 lbs. of celery, save the leaves
1 medium onion, peeled
1 large ripe pear, peeled
4 cups chicken broth
1/2 teaspoon salt
1/4 teaspoon ground white pepper
1/2 teaspoon garlic powder

In a 2 quart stock pot, melt the butter. In a food processor, finely chop the celery, to make 4 cups. Then chop the onions and pear. Add the vegetables to the stock pot and cook over low heat for 20 minutes, stirring frequently to prevent browning. Add the chicken broth, salt, pepper and garlic powder and cook, covered, for 40 minutes more. Strain the broth into a medium-sized bowl. In a food processor, purée the vegetables. Pour the vegetables and broth back into the stock pot and heat through. Serve topped with celery leaves.

Chestnut

Yield: 4 servings
Cooking time: 45 minutes

3 tablespoons butter
1 celery stalk, chopped
1 carrot, chopped
1/2 medium onion, chopped
1/4 teaspoon dried thyme leaves

4 cups chicken broth
1 (10-14 oz.) can or jar of vacuum
   packed chestnuts, chopped
1 teaspoon salt
1/2 teaspoon nutmeg

Melt the butter in a 4 quart stock pot. Add the celery, carrot, onion and thyme and sauté over medium heat for 10 minutes. Add the chicken broth, chestnuts, and salt. Bring to a boil, lower heat, cover, and simmer for 30 minutes. In a food processor, purée the soup in batches, being careful not to splatter the hot liquid. Return to the stock pot, stir in the nutmeg and reheat if necessary. Serve.

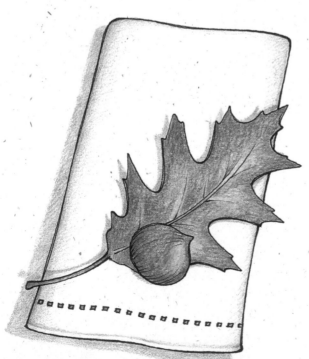

You can find canned chestnuts in specialty grocery stores year 'round. This soup makes a wonderful first course to an elegant dinner party.

Corn Chowder

Yield: 10 servings
Cooking time: 60 minutes

6 ears of corn, shucked
7 cups cold water
2 tablespoons olive oil
1 1/2 cups chopped onion
3/4 cup chopped red bell pepper
2 potatoes, peeled and cubed

2 teaspoons salt
1/4 teaspoon ground white pepper
1/8 to 1/4 teaspoon cayenne
 pepper
1/4 teaspoon ground thyme
1 cup half and half

Shuck the corn and set aside. Place the corn cobs into a 6 quart stock pot. Add the cold water. Bring to a boil, lower heat, cover and simmer for 10 minutes. Remove the cobs and set aside to cool. Pour the cooking broth into a large bowl and set aside. Heat the olive oil in the stock pot. Sauté the onion in the oil for 5 minutes. Stir in the chopped pepper and cook for 10 minutes. Stir in the cubed potatoes and cook for an additional 5 minutes. Add the 7 cups reserved corn broth, salt, pepper, cayenne, and ground thyme. Stir well. Bring to a boil, lower heat, cover and simmer for 30 minutes, until the potatoes are soft. In the meantime, remove the corn from the cobs. Discard the cobs. When the potatoes are cooked, stir in half of the corn. Next, purée the soup in batches in a food processor, being careful not to splatter the hot liquid. Return the purée to the stock pot. Stir in the remaining corn and the half and half. Heat through and serve.

Another terrific way to serve corn on the cob!

Eggplant Ratatouille

Yield: 8-10 servings
Cooking time: 60 minutes

3 tablespoons olive oil
2 cloves garlic
2 cups onion, chopped
1 bay leaf
1 medium eggplant, cubed
1 1/2 teaspoons salt
1 1/2 teaspoons basil
1 teaspoon marjoram
1/2 teaspoon rosemary

1/2 teaspoon thyme
1/2 teaspoon cumin
1/2 teaspoon fresh ground pepper
1 (28 oz.) can whole tomatoes
1 (6 oz.) can tomato paste
1 (13 3/4 oz.) can beef broth
1 (14.5 oz.) can vegetable broth
1 medium-sized zucchini, cubed
1 medium-sized bell pepper,
   chopped

In a 6 quart stock pot, heat the olive oil. Add the garlic, onion and bay leaf. Sauté over medium heat for 10 minutes until the onion is translucent. Add the eggplant, salt, basil, marjoram, rosemary, thyme and cumin. Stir well and cover. Cook over medium heat, stirring occasionally, for 20 minutes, or until the eggplant is soft. Add the pepper, tomatoes, tomato paste, beef broth and vegetable broth. Break up the whole tomatoes into smaller pieces with a spoon or knife. Bring to a boil. Cover and simmer for 20 minutes. Add the zucchini and bell pepper. Cover and simmer for 10 minutes until the zucchini and bell pepper are tender. Serve.

This recipe is another way ratatouille lovers can enjoy ratatouille!

Garlic

Yield: 6 servings
Cooking time: 60 minutes

3 tablespoons butter
8 medium garlic bulbs
2 medium onions
2 tablespoons parsley
2 (13.5 oz.) cans chicken broth
1 lemon

1/2 teaspoon ground thyme
1/4 teaspoon salt
1/4 teaspoon pepper
4 cups skim milk
1 tablespoon flour
French bread
Monterey Jack cheese

Separate garlic into cloves. You will have approximately 35-40 cloves. Peel and mince them. Melt the butter in a 4 quart stock pot. Add the onions, minced garlic and parsley. Sauté over medium heat for 10 minutes. Add the chicken broth, the juice from the lemon, thyme, salt and the pepper. Bring to a boil, lower heat, cover and simmer for 30 minutes. In a food processor, purée the soup in batches, being careful not to splatter the hot liquid. Return the purée to the pot. Stir in the milk and bring to a gentle boil. Stir often, being careful not to scald the milk. Stir in the flour. Reduce heat to low and simmer for 10 minutes. Prior to serving, toast several slices of the French bread. Pour the soup into ovenproof bowls. Top with a slice of bread and a slice of Monterey Jack cheese. Melt the cheese under the broiler. Serve.

This soup is for garlic lovers! It's the garlic version of onion soup.

Gazpacho

Yield: 8 serving
Cooking time: 2 hours

6 medium tomatoes, peeled and
  chopped
1 medium-sized onion, chopped
1 small green chili, seeded and chopped
1 garlic clove, chopped
1 1/2 teaspoons Worcestershire sauce
2 teaspoons salt
Dash Tabasco™ sauce
1/4 teaspoon freshly ground black
  pepper
1 medium-sized cucumber, peeled and
  chopped
1 small green pepper, seeded and
  chopped
1 large tomato, finely diced
1/4 cup chopped chives
2 lemons, cut into wedges

Place half of the chopped tomatoes, onion, green chili, garlic, Worcestershire sauce, salt, Tabasco™, and black pepper into a food processor or blender. Blend well. Slowly add the remaining chopped tomatoes. Blend well. Chill for 2 hours. Pour the mixture into a large bowl. Add the chopped cucumber, green pepper and diced tomato. Garnish with the chopped chives and serve with the lemon wedges.

This thick Gazpacho is the perfect first course on a hot summer evening.

Green Bean Potato

Yield: 10 servings
Cooking time: 1 hour 15 minutes

4 tablespoons butter
5 stalks celery, chopped
5 carrots, chopped
1 bunch green onions, chopped
1 small onion, chopped
3 tablespoons flour
2 quarts water
2 cups non-fat powdered milk

3 medium-sized potatoes, peeled
   and diced
1/4 teaspoon salt
1/4 teaspoon ground white pepper
1/2 cup chopped parsley
1 tablespoon Herbs de Provence
1 1/2 cups non-fat sour cream
1 (10 oz.) package frozen French
   style green beans

Melt the butter in a 6 quart stock pot. Sauté the celery, carrots, and onions for 15 minutes. Stir in the flour. Gradually stir in the water and then the powdered milk. Cook over medium heat until thickened, about 10 minutes. Add the diced potatoes, salt, pepper, parsley and Herbs de Provence. Simmer, stirring frequently, until the potatoes are tender, about 30 minutes. Stir in the sour cream, blending well. Add the green beans. Simmer for 20 more minutes. Serve.

Herbs de Provence can be purchased at any gourmet food store. It is a combination of many herbs--rosemary, thyme, marjoram, etc. You can use any of these by themselves as a substitute.

Horseradish

Yield: 6 servings
Cooking time: 1 hour 10 minutes

1 tablespoon butter
9 green onions, finely diced
3 (14.5 oz.) cans vegetable broth
3 large russet potatoes, peeled
   and cubed

1 1/4 cups fresh horseradish,
   peeled and grated
1/2 teaspoon salt
Dash white pepper

Melt the butter in a 2 quart stock pot. Add the green onions and sauté for 3 minutes. Add the vegetable broth, potatoes and horseradish. Bring to a boil, reduce heat, cover and simmer for 1 hour. Purée the soup in batches in the blender, being careful not to splatter the hot liquid. Return the soup to the stock pot. Season with salt and pepper. Heat through and serve.

The milder taste of fresh horseradish, combined with potatoes, creates a wonderful soup to serve as a first course for dinner.

Mushroom Barley

Yield: 8-10 servings
Cooking time: 60 minutes

1/2 oz. dried porcini mushrooms
3 tablespoons unsalted butter
1 onion, finely chopped
1 carrot, finely chopped
1/2 lb. fresh mushrooms, thinly
   sliced
10 cups beef stock

1 1/2 cups pearl barley, rinsed
   under cold water
1 bay leaf
1/2 teaspoon celery salt
1/4 teaspoon salt
1/4 teaspoon freshly ground
   pepper
2 tablespoons sherry

Put the porcini mushrooms in a small bowl and add lukewarm water to cover. Soak until softened, 15-30 minutes. Pour the porcini and the liquid through a strainer, reserving the liquid. Finely chop the porcini and set aside.

In a 6 quart stock pot, melt the butter over medium heat. Add the onion and carrot. Sauté until the onion is translucent, 2-3 minutes. Add the sliced fresh mushrooms, raise the heat and sauté until the mushrooms begin to soften, 2-3 minutes more. Add the stock, barley, bay leaf, and reserved porcini and soaking liquid. Bring to a boil. Reduce the heat to low, cover partially, and simmer gently, stirring occasionally, until the barley is tender, 50-60 minutes. Discard the bay leaf. Season with celery salt, salt and pepper. Stir in 2 tablespoons of sherry. Serve.

Enjoy the rich flavor of porcini mushrooms in this beef stock-based recipe.

Potato

Yield: 6 servings
Cooking time: 40 minutes

2 quarts water
6 medium-sized potatoes, diced
2 carrots, diced
3 celery stalks, diced
4 tablespoons flour

1 cup milk
2 teaspoons salt
1/4 teaspoon ground white
    pepper
Chive garnish

Pour the water into a 6 quart stock pot. Add the diced potatoes, carrots, and celery. Bring the water to a boil and cook for 20 minutes, until the potatoes are tender. Strain the vegetables, reserving the liquid. Place half of the vegetables into a food processor and purée. Add the flour and 1/2 cup of the reserved liquid. Blend. Return the other half of the vegetables to the stock pot. Stir in the potato purée and 1 cup milk. Add the salt and pepper. Heat through, being careful not to scald the milk. If soup is too thick, add more of the reserved liquid. Garnish with chives. Serve.

Serve this thick potato soup with a green salad and you have a delicious vegetarian meal.

Roasted Red Pepper

Yield: 6 servings
Cooking time: 1 hour 30 minutes

2 lbs. red peppers (6-7)
3 tablespoons olive oil
1 1/2 cups onion, chopped
1 cup chicken broth
2 cups water

1 teaspoon salt
Pinch of cayenne pepper
2 tablespoons lemon juice
6 fresh basil leaves, chopped

Cut peppers in half lengthwise. Remove stems, seeds and ribs. Lay cut side down on a baking sheet. Place under the broiler. Roast for 20 minutes, until skins blister and blacken. Remove and cover with tin foil. Let cool for 15 minutes. After the peppers have cooled, peel off the skins, and discard them. Chop the peppers into medium-sized pieces.

In the meantime, heat the oil in a 4 quart stock pot. Add the onion and sauté for 10 minutes. Add the chicken broth, water, salt and cayenne pepper. Bring to a boil, cover and simmer for 20 minutes. Add the roasted peppers and cook for 15 minutes over medium heat. Strain the peppers and onions, reserving the liquid. In a food processor, purée the peppers and onions in batches. Return the purée and reserved liquid to the stock pot. Add the lemon juice and basil and cook for 10 minutes. Serve.

Roasting and preparing the red peppers takes a little work, but the flavor is well worth it.

Sweet Potato Bisque

Yield: 6 servings
Cooking time: 40 minutes

1/2 cup butter
1/2 cup chopped onions
1 cup chopped celery
2 large sweet potatoes, peeled
   and diced

3 cups chicken broth
1 cup milk
1/2 teaspoon cloves
Salt and pepper to taste

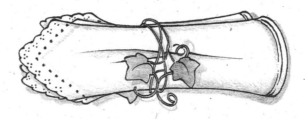

In a 4 quart stock pot, melt the butter. Add the onions and celery and sauté for 10 minutes. Add the diced sweet potatoes and chicken broth. Bring to a boil, lower heat to medium high, cover and cook for 25 minutes until the potatoes are very tender. In a food processor, purée the potatoes in batches, being careful not to splatter the hot liquid. Return the purée to the stock pot. Stir in the milk and cloves. Season to taste with salt and pepper. Reheat and serve.

This recipe showcases the wonderful flavor of sweet potato!

Southwestern Corn Chowder

Yield: 6 servings
Cooking time: 40 minutes

2 tablespoons olive oil
2 medium onions, minced
1 garlic clove, minced
1 jalapeno pepper, seeded and
   chopped
1 large sweet potato, peeled and
   thinly sliced
3 1/2 cups chicken broth

1/2 teaspoon ground cumin
1/4 teaspoon rubbed sage
3/4 cup sour cream
1 (14.5 oz.) can diced tomatoes
1 small zucchini, diced
2 ears of corn, shucked and cut
   off the cob
1 (16 oz.) can hominy, drained

In a 6 quart stock pot, heat olive oil. Sauté the onions, garlic and jalapeno pepper for 8 minutes. Add the sweet potato, 2 cups chicken broth, cumin and sage. Bring to a boil, cover, reduce heat to medium high and cook for 15 minutes, until the potatoes are soft. In a food processor, purée the soup in batches, being careful not to splatter the hot liquid. Return to the pan and stir in the sour cream. Add the diced tomatoes, zucchini, corn and hominy. Over medium heat, cook gently for 10 minutes, until the vegetables are tender but crisp. Serve.

The flavors of yellow and white corn are accompanied by sweet potato and zucchini in this vegetable chowder.

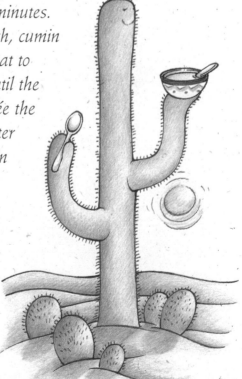

41

Southern Vegetable

Yield: 6 servings
Cooking time: 30 minutes

2 teaspoons olive oil
2 garlic cloves, minced
1 medium-sized onion, diced
1 cup diced red potatoes
1/2 teaspoon salt
1/8 teaspoon ground white pepper
1/2 teaspoon savory
1/2 teaspoon tarragon leaves

1 (28 oz.) can crushed tomatoes
3 (14.5 oz.) cans vegetable broth
1 (16 oz.) package frozen country
  blend vegetables
1 (4 oz.) can diced green chilies,
  drained
1 cup sliced okra

Heat the oil in a 4 quart stock pot over medium-high heat. Add the garlic and onion and sauté for 5 minutes. Add the diced potatoes and sauté for 5 minutes. Stir in the salt, white pepper, savory and tarragon leaves. Add the crushed tomatoes and vegetable broth. Bring to a boil.

Add the frozen vegetables, green chilies and okra. Reduce heat, cover and simmer for 20 minutes. Serve.

This vegetable soup recipe is spiced up with green chilies and okra.

Squash Apple

Yield: 4 servings
Cooking time: 35 minutes

2 lb. acorn squash
1/3 cup chopped onion
1/3 cup chopped carrot
1 3/4 cups apple juice
1 chicken bouillon cube

1 teaspoon lemon juice
1/8 teaspoon ground ginger
1/8 teaspoon white pepper
1/3 cup skim milk
1/4 cup sour cream (optional)

To cook the squash: Cut it in half and cook in a 450 degree oven for 1 hour until soft. Or quarter the squash, put it into a glass cooking pan with 1/4 cup water, cover and microwave on high for 15 minutes until soft. In a large saucepan, cook the onion and carrot in the apple juice, with the chicken bouillon cube, covered for 12 minutes until tender. Stir in the lemon juice, ginger and pepper. Slowly pour the hot liquid into the food processor and purée with the squash. Return the mixture to the saucepan. Add the skim milk and bring to a gentle boil. Reduce heat, cover and simmer for 5 minutes until the flavors are blended. Serve with a dollop of sour cream on top.

The name of this recipe and the ingredients bring to mind the sensational flavors and feelings of the fall season.

Fresh Tomato

Yield: 6 servings
Cooking time: 60 minutes

4 lbs. tomatoes, peeled
2 stalks celery, chopped
1/4 cup onion, chopped
1 teaspoon sugar
1 teaspoon salt
1 tablespoon parsley flakes

1/4 teaspoon thyme leaves
1/2 teaspoon basil leaves
2 (14.5 oz.) cans vegetable broth
1 (6 oz.) can tomato paste
1 teaspoon lemon juice

To peel the tomatoes, drop them into a pot of boiling water. Boil for 2 minutes until the skins split open. Remove from the water, cool slightly, and peel off the skins and chop them.

In a 4 quart stock pot, combine the chopped tomatoes, celery, onion, sugar, salt, parsley flakes, thyme and basil. Cook over medium heat for 20 minutes. In a food processor, purée the vegetables in batches. Return to the stock pot. Add the vegetable broth, tomato paste and lemon juice. Cook over medium heat for 15 minutes. Serve.

Garden-ripe tomatoes make this recipe a winner!

Tomato Rice

Yield: 6 servings
Cooking time: 35 minutes

1 tablespoon olive oil
1 medium-sized onion,
   chopped
2 garlic cloves, minced
1/2 cup long grain rice
3 cups chicken broth
4 lbs. fresh plum tomatoes
1 teaspoon basil
1 teaspoon marjoram
3 teaspoons sugar
1 teaspoon salt
1/4 teaspoon ground black
   pepper
2 tablespoons chopped fresh
   parsley

Heat the oil in a 4 quart
stock pot. Add the onion and garlic and
sauté for 5 minutes. Stir in the rice and
cook for 2 minutes, stirring constantly.
Add the chicken broth and turn the heat
to high. Coarsely chop the tomatoes
and then purée them in a food processor. Stir into the soup. Add the basil,
marjoram, sugar, salt and pepper. Stir
well. Bring to a boil, lower heat, cover
and simmer for 30 minutes. Stir in the
parsley and serve.

Tomatoes and rice--food for the soul.

Garden Vegetable

Yield: 12 servings
Cooking time: 40 minutes

1 tablespoon butter
1 medium onion, diced
1 garlic clove, diced
2 medium carrots, sliced
5 (14.5 oz.) cans vegetable broth
1 celery stalk, sliced
4 new potatoes, sliced
2 teaspoons salt
1 teaspoon ground white pepper
1/2 teaspoon ground oregano
1/2 teaspoon celery salt
1 zucchini, sliced
1 cup green beans, cut into
   1 inch pieces
6 plum tomatoes, sliced
1 cup frozen peas
1 (28 oz.) can crushed tomatoes
1 cup fresh parsley, chopped

In a 6 quart stock pot, melt the butter. Sauté the onion and garlic for 5 minutes. Add the vegetable broth, carrots, celery, potatoes, salt, pepper, oregano and celery salt. Bring to a boil, lower heat, and simmer for 20 minutes. Add the zucchini, green beans, plum tomatoes, peas, crushed tomatoes and parsley. Simmer for 15 minutes. Serve.

You can add any vegetables and seasonings to this basic recipe. Experiment!

Vichyssoise

Yield: 8 servings
Cooking time: 50 minutes

5 leeks, (white part) chopped fine
1 medium onion, chopped fine
2 tablespoons butter
5 medium potatoes, diced
1 quart chicken broth
1 tablespoon salt
1/2 teaspoon ground white pepper
2 cups milk
2 cups half and half
1 cup heavy cream
Chopped chives

In a 6 quart stock pot, lightly brown the leeks and onion in the butter. Add the potatoes, chicken broth, salt, and pepper. Bring to a boil and cook for 40 minutes. Remove from the heat and carefully blend in a food processor or blender. Return to the stock pot and add the 2 cups milk and 2 cups half and half. Bring to a gentle boil and then remove from heat. If the potatoes are lumpy, run through the food processor again. Cool for at least two hours or overnight in the refrigerator. When the soup is cold, stir in the cream. Serve topped with chopped chives.

The name may not be easy to pronounce, but the recipe is easy to make and very delicious!

Wild Rice and Shiitake Mushroom

Yield: 6 servings
Cooking time: 60 minutes

4 oz. wild rice
6 cups water
1 1/2 tablespoons olive oil
1/2 cup chopped shallots
1/2 cup chopped celery
1 cup sliced shiitake mushrooms
1/4 teaspoon ground black pepper
1/4 teaspoon ground white pepper

1/8 teaspoon thyme
1/2 teaspoon ground coriander
1/4 teaspoon rosemary
1/8 teaspoon salt
1/8 teaspoon garlic powder
1 tablespoon parsley flakes
1 cup chicken broth

In a medium-sized bowl, soak the rice in 2 cups of water. In a 4 quart stock pot, sauté celery and shallots in olive oil until onions are clear. Pour the rice and soaking water into the stock pot. Add the rest of the ingredients and bring to a boil. Cover and simmer for 1 hour. Serve.

The nutty, earthy flavor of wild rice and shiitake mushrooms are showcased in this wonderful soup.

Hearty Beans and Crock Cookery

Black Bean

Yield: 8-10 servings
Cooking time: 3 hours 30 minutes

1 (16 oz.) package dried black
  beans
6 cups water
2 ham hocks
1 1/2 cups chopped onions
2 cups chopped celery
1 cup chopped carrots
1 bay leaf
2 cloves
1/2 teaspoon dry mustard
Freshly ground pepper

The night before, place the black beans into a medium-sized bowl. Cover with water and soak overnight.

The next day, drain the water and put the beans into a 4 quart stock pot. Add 6 cups of water and the ham hocks. Bring to a boil, lower heat, cover and simmer for 2 hours. Add the onions, celery, carrots, bay leaf, cloves and mustard. Simmer, covered, for 1 1/2 hours. Remove ham hocks, bay leaf and cloves. In a food processor, purée half of the black beans. Note: some people prefer to purée all of the beans. Stir puréed beans into the rest of the soup. Season with freshly ground pepper and serve.

Serve this hearty black bean soup with crusty bread and you have a meal!

Escarole and White Bean

Yield: 6 servings
Cooking time: 1 hour 5 minutes

1 1/2 cups dried northern beans
2 slices bacon, cut in 1/4 inch pieces
1/2 cup chopped onion
1/2 lb. mushrooms, cleaned and
 sliced
1 garlic clove, chopped

2 quarts chicken broth
1 teaspoon salt
1/2 teaspoon ground white pepper
1/4 teaspoon ground thyme
1 1/2 lbs. escarole
Parmesan cheese

The night before, place the beans into a medium-sized bowl. Cover with water and soak overnight. The next day, drain the water and set the beans aside.

In a 4 quart stock pot, brown the bacon. Add the onion, mushrooms, and garlic and sauté for 10 minutes. Add a little olive oil if you need more cooking oil. Add the chicken broth, salt, pepper, thyme and the beans. Bring to a boil, lower heat, cover and cook for 40 minutes. Clean the escarole and tear into large pieces. Add to the soup and simmer gently for 15 minutes. Serve with a garnish of Parmesan cheese.

The chicken broth base and the escarole lend a lighter feel to this bean soup.

Garbanzo Bean

Yield: 10 servings
Cooking time: 2 hours 20 minutes

12 oz. dried chick peas
3 tablespoons olive oil
1 large onion, chopped
1 cup chopped celery
2 garlic cloves, minced

1 (28 oz.) can crushed tomatoes
6 cups chicken broth
1/2 small head cabbage, shredded
1 tablespoon parsley flakes
1/2 teaspoon ground cumin

The night before, place the chick peas into a medium-sized bowl. Cover with water and soak overnight.

The next day, drain the water and put the chick peas into a 6 quart stock pot. Cover with fresh water an inch over the level of the chick peas. Bring to a boil, lower heat, and simmer covered for 1 1/2 hours. Drain and set aside in a bowl. Heat the olive oil in the same stock pot. Add the onion, celery and garlic and sauté 5 minutes. Add the tomatoes, chicken broth and chick-peas. Stir well. Bring to a boil, lower heat, and simmer covered for 30 minutes. Add the cabbage, parsley and cumin. Cook covered for 15 minutes longer. Serve.

 This soup has an exotic Middle Eastern flair.

Lentil

Yield: 10 servings
Cooking time: 1 hour 15 minutes

2 cups dried lentils
8 cups water
2 teaspoons salt
1 cup chopped onion
1/2 cup chopped celery

1/2 cup chopped carrots
1/2 teaspoon ground thyme
1/2 teaspoon ground pepper
2 beef bouillon cubes

In a 4 quart stock pot, place the lentils, 7 cups of water and salt. Bring to a boil, lower heat and simmer, partially covered for 30 minutes. Stir in the onion, celery, carrots, thyme, and pepper. In a microwave, bring the remaining cup of water to a boil. Dissolve the beef bouillon cubes. Add to the stock pot. Partially cover and simmer for 45 minutes, stirring occasionally. Serve.

A great down-home recipe to serve for lunch or dinner.

Lima Bean

Yield: 6 servings
Cooking time: 2 hours 10 minutes

2 cups dried lima beans
4 (14.5 oz.) cans vegetable broth
3 tablespoons olive oil
1 large onion, coarsely chopped
1 cup chopped celery
2 garlic cloves, minced

1 large potato, diced
1 1/2 cups tomato purée
1 cup tomato juice
2 tablespoons chopped chives
1 tablespoon minced basil

The night before, soak the lima beans in a medium-sized bowl. The next day, drain the beans.

In a 4 quart stock pot, bring the vegetable broth to a boil. Add the lima beans, lower heat, cover and simmer for 1 1/2 hours. Heat the olive oil in a skillet. Add the onion, celery and garlic and sauté for 10 minutes. Transfer the vegetables to the soup. Add the potato, tomato purée, and tomato juice.
Return the soup to a boil, lower heat, cover, and simmer 25 minutes. Stir in the chives and basil. Simmer 5 minutes. Serve.

Lima beans take the spotlight in this recipe.

Split Pea

Yield: 12 servings
Cooking time: 3 hours

1 lb. dried peas
1 (46 oz.) can unsalted
 chicken broth
1 1/2 lbs. ham hock
2 cups chopped onion
2 cups chopped carrots
2 cups chopped celery
2 bay leaves
Salt and ground pepper

In a 6 quart stock pot, combine the dried peas, chicken broth and ham hocks. Bring to a boil. Add the onion, carrot, celery and bay leaves. Stir. Cover and simmer for 3 hours. Remove the bay leaves and the ham hock. Remove the meat from the bone and chop it into small pieces. Carefully purée the peas, in 3 cup batches, in a blender or food processor. Be careful not to splatter the hot liquid. Return the purée to the stock pot and add the ham pieces. Add salt and pepper to taste. Heat through and serve with croutons on top.

I love a very thick pea soup and this recipe fits the bill.

White Bean Chowder

Yield: 10 servings
Cooking time: 2 hours

1/2 lb. dried navy beans
1 tablespoon olive oil
1 large onion, finely chopped
2 cloves garlic, minced
1 quart water
2 (14.5 oz.) cans chicken broth
1 bay leaf
4 cups potatoes, peeled and diced

2 (14.5 oz.) cans diced tomatoes
1 (6 oz.) can tomato paste
1/2 teaspoon dried thyme
1/2 teaspoon ground oregano
1 teaspoon salt
1 teaspoon ground black pepper
2 medium-sized zucchini, sliced

The night before, place the beans into a medium-sized bowl. Cover with water and soak overnight.

The next day, drain the water and set the beans aside. In a 6 quart stock pot heat the olive oil. Add the chopped onion and the garlic. Cook for 10 minutes over medium heat until the onion is translucent. Add the beans, water, chicken broth, bay leaf and diced potatoes. Bring to a boil. Reduce heat, cover and simmer for 1 hour.

Add the diced tomatoes, tomato paste, thyme, oregano, salt, and pepper. Simmer, covered, for 30 minutes. Add the zucchini and simmer for 10-15 minutes until it is tender. Serve.

Take navy beans, add zucchini and potatoes and what do you get? A delicious chowder.

Navy Bean Vegetable

Yield: 12 servings
Cooking time: 3 hours

1 lb. dried navy beans
6 cups water
1 (28 oz.) can whole tomatoes
1 (8 oz.) can tomato paste
1 cup chopped carrots
1 cup chopped onions
1 cup chopped celery
1/4 teaspoon garlic powder
2 bay leaves

1 1/2 teaspoons salt
1/2 teaspoon ground white
    pepper
1 chicken bouillon cube
Dash thyme
Dash ground cloves
1 tablespoon hot sauce (or more to
    your taste)

The night before, place the beans into a large bowl. Cover with water and soak overnight.

The next day, drain the water and put the beans into a 6 quart stock pot. Add 3 cups of water and boil for 1 1/2 hours. Roughly chop the whole tomatoes in the can and add to the beans, with 3 additional cups of water. Stir in the tomato paste and the rest of the ingredients. Simmer uncovered for 1 1/2 hours. Remove the bay leaves and serve.

No matter the size of your family, prepare this recipe and you'll be surprised how fast it disappears.

Cabbage and Beef

Yield: 6-8 servings
Cooking time: Low setting 8-10 hours
High setting 5-7 hours

2 lbs. beef brisket
2 stalks celery, diced
10 oz. dried pearl onions, skinned
1 quart water
3 beef bouillon cubes

1/4 teaspoon garlic powder
1/4 teaspoon ground pepper
1/2 cup red wine
1/2 medium-sized head cabbage,
  sliced

Cut the beef brisket into small chunks. Place into a 4 quart slow cooker. Add the celery and skinned onions. (To skin the onions, drop into boiling water for 2 minutes. Remove, cool and skin.) In the microwave, bring two cups of the water to a boil. Dissolve the bouillon in the water. Stir in the garlic powder and the pepper. Pour over the meat with the red wine. Place the cabbage on top of the meat and vegetables. Do not mix in with the rest of the ingredients. Add remaining 2 cups of water to cover. Cook on low setting for 8-10 hours or on high setting 5-7 hours. Serve.

Beef brisket slow cooked in wine with onions is a wonderful meal to come home to after a hard day's work.

Corned Beef and Cabbage

Yield: 6-8 servings
Cooking time: Low setting 8-10 hours
High setting 5-7 hours

2-3 lbs. corned beef
1 medium onion, sliced
2 potatoes, peeled and sliced

1 quart water
2 teaspoons salt
1 teaspoon ground pepper
1/4 small head cabbage, sliced

Cut the corned beef into small chunks. Place into a 4 quart slow cooker. Sprinkle with the pickling spices included with the corned beef. Add the onion slices and the potatoes. Cover with water. Sprinkle with salt and pepper. Place the cabbage on top of the meat and vegetables. Do not mix in with the rest of the ingredients. Cook on low setting for 8-10 hours or on the high setting 5-7 hours. Serve.

 An Irish corned beef dinner cooked in one pot..

Five O'Clock Bean

Yield: 6-8 servings
Cooking time: Low setting 8-10 hours
High setting 5-7 hours

1/2 cup dried navy beans
1/2 cup dried northern beans
1/2 cup dried baby lima beans
1/2 cup dried yellow split beans
1/2 cup dried pinto beans
2 quarts water
2 stalks celery
1 carrot
1 cup chopped ham

2 teaspoons salt
1 teaspoon ground cumin
1 teaspoon ground white pepper
1 teaspoon garlic powder
2 beef bouillon cubes

The night before, combine all of the beans into a large bowl. Cover with water and soak overnight.

The next morning, drain the water and put the beans into a 4 quart crock pot. Add 2 quarts of water. Break the celery and carrot in two and add to the pot with the ham, salt, ground cumin, white pepper, garlic powder and bouillon cubes. Stir well. Cook on low setting for 8-10 hours. Remove the celery and carrot and serve.

A little preparation in the morning and this vegetarian dinner is ready when you get home from work.

Navy Bean and Ham

Yield: 6-8 servings
Cooking time: Low setting 8-10 hours
High setting 5-7 hours

1 lb. dried navy beans
6 cups water
1 cup chopped carrots
1 cup chopped celery
2 cups diced potatoes
1 teaspoon garlic powder
1 teaspoon minced onion

2 teaspoons salt
1/2 teaspoon ground white
pepper
1 cup diced smoked ham
2 chicken bouillon cubes
1 tablespoon chopped chives

The night before, put the beans into a large bowl. Cover with water and soak overnight.

The next morning, drain the water and put the beans into a 4 quart crock pot. Add 6 cups of water, the carrots, celery, potatoes, garlic powder, minced onion, salt, pepper, smoked ham, bouillon cubes and chives. Stir well.

Cook on low setting for 8-10 hours.

The flavors in this soup are even better the next day.

Vegetable Beef

Yield: 8 servings
Cooking time: Low setting 8-10 hours
High setting 5-7 hours

1 lb. beef stew chunks
2 ears of corn
1 medium onion, chopped
1 cup green beans, chopped
1 cup chopped celery
1 cup chopped carrots
1 cup chopped zucchini
1 cup chopped baby squash
1 cup diced potatoes
1 (28 oz.) can crushed tomatoes
1 tablespoon salt
1/4 teaspoon ground black pepper
1 1/2 teaspoons Worcestershire sauce
2 teaspoons dried parsley flakes

Cut beef into bite-size pieces and place into a 4 quart crock pot. Remove the corn from the ears and add to the beef with all of the ingredients. Add water to cover, about 2 cups. Stir well. Cover and cook on low setting for 8 to 10 hours.

Come home from work to the wonderful aroma and taste of this soup!

Lamb and Bean

Yield: 6-8 servings
Cooking time: Low setting 8-10 hours
High setting 5-7 hours

3/4 cup dried navy beans	1 large onion, chopped
3/4 cup dried baby lima beans	2 carrots, chopped
3 (13.75 oz.) cans beef broth	3 whole tomatoes, chopped
2-3 lb. seasoned lamb shoulder	1 large zucchini, chopped

The night before, put the beans into a large bowl. Cover with water and soak overnight.

The next morning, drain the water and put the beans into a 4 quart crock pot. Add the beef broth, seasoned lamb shoulder, onion, carrots, tomatoes and zucchini. Cook on low setting for 8-10 hours. Serve.
Note: Remove the string tied around the lamb before cooking.

You can find seasoned lamb shoulder at your local grocery store. Throw it in a pot with a few other ingredients and when you get home, you'll have a very flavorful soup!

Main Dish Soups

Beef Barley

Yield: 10 servings
Cooking time: 2 hours 30 minutes

2 to 3 lb. chuck roast
1 (28 oz.) can whole tomatoes,
  crushed
1 (8 oz.) can tomato paste
1 cup water
1 cup chopped celery
1 cup chopped carrots
1 cup chopped onion

1 teaspoon salt
1/2 teaspoon ground black
  pepper
1/8 teaspoon thyme
1/2 teaspoon garlic powder
2 bay leaves
1/2 cup barley

Trim any fat from the chuck roast and place it in a 6 quart stock pot. Stir together the crushed tomatoes, tomato paste, and water in stock pot. Add the rest of the ingredients, except for the barley, and cook covered for 2 hours. Add the barley and cook for 1/2 hour longer. Add more water if necessary. Remove the bay leaves and serve.

The aroma of this soup cooking on the stove will have your family at the dinner table on time!

Beef Noodle

Yield: 10 servings
Cooking time: 40 minutes

1 1/2 lbs. beef sirloin tip steak
3 tablespoons olive oil
1 cup chopped onion
1 cup chopped celery
1 cup chopped carrots
1 garlic clove, chopped
1 teaspoon salt

1/2-1 teaspoon ground black
  pepper
4 (13.75 oz.) cans beef broth
1 tablespoon soy sauce
2 cups dried egg noodles
1 (17 oz.) can sweet peas
1 tablespoon dried parsley

Slice the beef sirloin tip steak into thin strips, 1 inch long. Heat the olive oil in a 4 quart stock pot. Add the beef and sauté over medium-high heat for 15 minutes, stirring constantly, until the beef is browned. Add the onions, celery, carrots, garlic, salt and pepper and sauté for 5 minutes. Add the beef broth and soy sauce and bring to a boil. Reduce heat, cover and simmer for 15 minutes. Fill a 2 quart saucepan with water and bring it to a boil. Add the egg noodles and cook for 10 minutes until the noodles are tender. Add the noodles, peas and parsley to the soup. Cook for 5 minutes and serve.

Your family won't have to wait long to dish into this soup!

Beef Stroganoff

Yield: 4 servings
Cooking time: 30 minutes

2 teaspoons olive oil
1 lb. sliced mushrooms
1 lb. pepper steak
1/2 teaspoon minced garlic
1 teaspoon salt
1/2 teaspoon ground black pepper

1/2 cup red wine
4 cups water
2 beef bouillon cubes
1 (16 oz.) jar whole small
   onions, drained
Optional: 1/2 cup cooked egg
   noodles

   Heat the olive oil in a 2 quart stock pot. Add the sliced mushrooms and sauté for 5 minutes. Slice the pepper steak into thin slices, 1 1/2 inches long. Add the steak to the mushrooms with the garlic, salt, and black pepper. Sauté for 10 minutes. In the meantime, heat the water to the boiling point in the microwave or in a saucepan. Dissolve the bouillon cubes in the hot water. Stir the red wine into the meat. Add the beef broth and the onions. Bring to a boil, cover and simmer for 15 minutes. If adding egg noodles, stir in now. Serve.

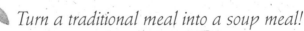 Turn a traditional meal into a soup meal!

Oriental Beef

Enjoy a bowl of Oriental Beef S... #6

Yield: 4 servings
Cooking time: 45 minutes

2 tablespoons soy sauce
1 teaspoon ground ginger
1/4 teaspoon crushed red pepper
3/4 lb. boneless beef top sirloin
   steak, 1 inch thick
1 tablespoon vegetable oil

2 cups sliced fresh mushrooms
2 (14 oz.) cans beef broth
1/2 cup water
1 cup fresh snow peas, cut
   diagonally into 1 inch pieces
1 tablespoon minced onion

Combine soy sauce, ginger and crushed red pepper in a small bowl. Spread evenly over both sides of the steak. Marinate at room temperature for 15 minutes.

Pour oil into a 4 quart stock pot. Over a medium-high setting, heat oil until hot. Drain the steak, reserving marinade. Cook the steak in the stock pot for 5 minutes per side for medium-rare. Adjust cooking time for desired doneness. Remove steak and let it stand, covered, on a cutting board for 10 minutes. Add mushrooms to the stock pot and stir-fry for 2 minutes. Add the broth, water, peas, minced onion, and remaining marinade. Bring to a boil, scraping up browned meat bits. Reduce heat to low. Cut steak across the grain into 1/8 inch slices. Cut each slice into 1 inch pieces. Stir into soup and heat through. Serve.

Lasagne

Yield: 6 servings
Cooking time: 50 minutes

4 oz. Italian sausage
4 stalks celery, diced
1 small onion, diced
1 large garlic clove, minced
5 large mushrooms, chopped
1 (28 oz.) can tomatoes, chopped
1 (15 oz.) can tomato purée
3 chicken bouillon cubes
1 beef bouillon cube
4 cups water

1 teaspoon basil
1 teaspoon oregano
1/2 teaspoon thyme
1/2 teaspoon crushed red pepper
8 lasagne noodles
2 cups ricotta cheese
1/2 cup shredded mozzarella
   cheese
Parmesan cheese

Remove the sausage from the casing. Crumble into a 4 quart stock pot and cook until browned. Add the onion, celery, garlic and mushrooms. Sauté the vegetables for 5 minutes. Add the chopped tomatoes, tomato purée, bouillon cubes, water, basil, oregano, thyme and crushed red pepper. Bring to a boil, reduce heat, and simmer, uncovered, for 30 minutes. Break the lasagne noodles into pieces and add to the soup. Cook over medium heat until the noodles are tender, about 15 minutes. Serve topped with ricotta, mozzarella and Parmesan cheese.

The next time you face hours making lasagne, try this easy soup recipe.

Southern Short Rib

Yield: 6 servings
Cooking time: 3 hours 50 minutes

1 cup dried pinto beans
2 lbs. short ribs
12 cups water
2 onions, quartered
1 carrot, halved
1 stalk celery, halved
1 bay leaf
6 peppercorns
1/4 teaspoon dried thyme leaves
2 tablespoons olive oil

1 medium-sized onion, chopped
2 garlic cloves, minced
1/2 cup brown rice
1 cup tomato juice
1 tablespoon Worcestershire sauce
3 teaspoons beef bouillon
1 teaspoon salt
1 teaspoon pepper
2 parsnips, diced
1/4 cup finely chopped parsley

The night before, place the pinto beans into a small bowl. Cover with water and soak overnight. The next day, drain the pinto beans and set aside.

Place the short ribs into a 6 quart stock pot. Add the water and bring it to a boil. Lower the heat to a simmer and add the onions, carrot, celery, bay leaf, peppercorns, and thyme. Partially cover and simmer gently for 2 hours, until the meat is tender. Strain the soup and degrease the broth. Return the broth to the stock pot. Remove the meat from the short ribs and trim off the fat. Slice the meat thinly and return it to the stock pot. Add the pinto beans to the pot. Bring it to a boil, lower heat, cover and simmer for 1 hour.

In the meantime, heat the olive oil in a skillet. Add the onion and sauté for 5 minutes. Add the garlic and rice. Cook, stirring constantly, on medium-high heat, for 5 minutes. Transfer the rice mixture to the stock pot. Stir in the tomato juice, Worcestershire sauce, beef bouillon, salt and pepper. Return to a boil, lower heat, cover, and simmer 20 minutes.
Add the parsnips and parsley. Cook for 30 more minutes. Serve.

Oxtail

Yield: 10 servings
Cooking time: 5 hours 30 minutes

2 lb. oxtails or veal tails
Flour
2 tablespoons vegetable oil
1 medium-sized onion, sliced
8 cups water
1 teaspoon salt
4 peppercorns
1/4 cup chopped fresh parsley

1 large carrot, diced
1 stalk celery, diced
1 bay leaf
1 (28 oz.) can crushed tomatoes
1 teaspoon dried thyme
2 tablespoons butter
2 tablespoons flour
1/4 cup Madeira sherry

Roll the oxtails in the flour. Heat the oil in a 4 quart stock pot. Brown the oxtails with the onions in the oil. Add the water, salt, and peppercorns. Bring to a boil, lower heat and simmer, uncovered for 5 hours. Add the parsley, carrots, celery, bay leaf, tomatoes

and thyme. Simmer for 1/2 hour until the vegetables are tender. Strain the broth and remove the bay leaf, peppercorns and oxtails. Cut the meat from the bone and discard the bones. In a food processor, purée the broth, vegetables and meat together in batches, being careful not to splatter the hot liquid. Return to the stock pot. Melt the butter in a small saucepan. Stir in the flour and make a paste. Stir the paste into the soup with the Madeira sherry. Heat through and serve.

If oxtails are not available at your grocery store, oxjoints or veal tails can be substituted. The long hours of cooking make the meat tender and the flavors extra good in this soup.

75

Italian Sausage with Tortellini

Yield: 12 servings
Cooking time: 1 hour 10 minutes

1 lb. Italian sausage
1 cup chopped onions
2 garlic cloves, minced
3 (13 3/4 oz.) cans beef broth
1/2 cup dry red wine
1 (28 oz.) can crushed tomatoes
1 (28 oz.) can peeled whole
   tomatoes, cut up
1 (15 oz.) can tomato sauce
1 cup sliced carrots
1/2 teaspoon dried basil
1/2 teaspoon dried oregano
1 tablespoon parsley flakes
1 cup sliced zucchini
9 oz. package of fresh cheese-filled
   tortellini
1 medium-sized green bell pepper,
   chopped
Parmesan cheese

Remove the casing from the sausage. In a 6 quart stock pot, brown the sausage over medium heat. Set aside, reserving drippings in stock pot. Cook the onions and garlic in the sausage drippings for about 10 minutes. Add the cooked sausage, beef broth, red wine, crushed tomatoes, whole tomatoes, tomato sauce, carrots, basil, oregano, and parsley flakes. Stir well and bring to a boil. Reduce heat and simmer, covered for 30 minutes. Stir in the zucchini, tortellini, and bell pepper. Cover and simmer for 20 to 25 minutes until the tortellini are tender. Sprinkle each serving with Parmesan cheese.

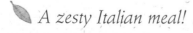 A zesty Italian meal!

Pinto Bean and Sausage

Yield: 6 servings
Cooking time: 1 hour 50 minutes

1 1/2 cups dried pinto beans
1 tablespoon butter
1 medium-sized onion, chopped
2 celery stalks, chopped
1 garlic clove, minced
2 (13.75 oz.) cans beef broth
2 cups tomato juice
3 turnips, diced
2 carrots, diced
1/2 teaspoon dried oregano
1/2 teaspoon black pepper

1/2 lb. smoked sausage, cut into
thin slices and then diced
1/4 cup chopped fresh parsley

The night before, place the pinto beans into a small bowl. Cover with water and soak overnight. The next day, drain the pinto beans and set aside.

Melt the butter in a 6 quart stock pot. Add the onion and celery and sauté for 5 minutes. Add the garlic and sauté for 1 minute. Add the beef broth, tomato juice and pinto beans. Bring to a boil, lower heat and simmer for 1 hour and 15 minutes. Add the turnips, carrots, oregano and pepper. Simmer, covered for 30 minutes. Add the sausage and parsley. Cook for 5 minutes until the sausage is heated through. Serve.

Sweet Potato and Sausage

Yield: 6 servings
Cooking time: 30 minutes

1/2 lb. smoked sausage, cut into
   1/2-inch slices
1 medium-sized sweet potato, peeled
   and cut into 1/2-inch cubes
1 cup coarsely shredded cabbage
1/2 cup chopped green pepper
1/2 cup chopped celery
1/2 cup chopped onion

1 (14.5 oz.) can diced tomatoes,
   undrained
1 (15.5 oz.) can blackeye peas,
   undrained
1 (13.75 oz.) can beef broth
1 cup tomato juice
1/2 teaspoon salt
1/4 teaspoon ground black pepper

In a 4-quart stock pot, combine all ingredients. Bring to a boil over medium-high heat. Cover, reduce heat, and simmer for 30 minutes, stirring occasionally. Serve.

This flavorful soup tastes like it takes hours to prepare, but is so easy to throw together!

Cheese and Creamed Soups

Cauliflower Cheese

Yield: 6 servings
Cooking time: 40 minutes

1 large cauliflower, cut into flowerets
1 large potato, peeled and diced
1 cup chopped onion
1 cup chopped carrot
1 clove garlic, minced
1 1/4 teaspoons salt

4 cups water
3/4 cup low-fat milk
2 cups grated sharp cheddar
  cheese
1 teaspoon dill

Reserve 2 cups of the cauliflower flowerets. In a 4 quart stock pot, place the remaining cauliflower flowerets, potato, onion, carrot, garlic, salt and water. Bring to a boil. Lower heat, cover and simmer for 20 minutes, until the vegetables are tender. In the meantime, steam the 2 cups cauliflower flowerets in a small saucepan for 15 minutes until tender. Set aside. In a food processor, purée the soup in batches, being careful not to splatter the hot liquid. Return the purée to the stock pot. Stir in the milk, cheese, dill and steamed cauliflower flowerets. Heat gently until the cheese is melted. Serve topped with an extra sprinkle of cheese.

Cheddar cheese enhances the distinctive flavor of cauliflower in this recipe.

Broccoli Cheddar Cheese

Yield: 6 servings
Cooking time: 30 minutes

2 tablespoons butter
1 cup chopped onion
1/4 cup flour
4 cups low-fat milk
1/2 teaspoon salt
1/4 teaspoon dry mustard

1/4 teaspoon basil leaves
1/2 teaspoon Worcestershire sauce
1/2 teaspoon ground white pepper
3 cups broccoli flowerets
1 lb. grated sharp cheddar cheese

Melt the butter in a 4 quart stock pot. Add the onion and sauté for 5 minutes. Stir in the flour and then half of the milk. Mix well. Add the rest of the milk, the salt, mustard, basil, Worcestershire sauce and pepper. Mix well. Add the broccoli flowerets. Over medium heat, bring the milk close to the boiling point. Cook for 20 minutes, being careful not to scald the milk. Stir often. Add the cheddar cheese and stir until it is melted, about 5 minutes. Serve.

For the broccoli and cheese lover!

Mexican Cheese

Yield: 10 servings
Cooking time: 30 minutes

1 lb. bacon
2 large onions, chopped
6 stalks celery, chopped
1 (28 oz.) can whole tomatoes, chopped

1 cup water
1 cup tomato juice
1 lb. shredded cheddar cheese
1 (14 oz.) can pinto beans

Cut the bacon into small pieces. In a 6 quart stock pot, fry the bacon until it is crispy. Remove the bacon, leaving the fat. Sauté the onions and celery in the bacon fat. Drain off any excess bacon grease. Add the chopped tomatoes, water, tomato juice and bacon. Bring to a boil, lower heat and add the shredded cheddar cheese. Simmer until the cheese is melted, stirring often. In the meantime, purée the pinto beans in a food processor or blender. Stir into the soup and heat through. If soup is too thick, it can be thinned with water or additional tomato juice.

Bacon, pinto beans and tomatoes create a very thick and flavorful cheese soup in this easy recipe.

Vermont Cheddar Cheese

Yield: 4 servings
Cooking time: 60 minutes

1 leek (white part only)
1 stalk celery
1/2 medium onion
3 cups chicken stock
2 tablespoons cornstarch
2 tablespoons water

1 cup shredded Vermont
   cheddar cheese
1/8 teaspoon white pepper
1/8 teaspoon nutmeg
Salt to taste
1 egg yolk
1/2 cup cream

   Chop the vegetables. Pour the chicken broth into a medium-sized
saucepan. Add the vegetables and bring to a boil. Lower the heat and
simmer, uncovered for 45 minutes. Strain the vegetables. In a small bowl,
mix the cornstarch and water to form a paste. Stir into the broth and cook
until slightly thickened. Add the cheese and cook until the cheese melts.
Add the white pepper and nutmeg, and salt to taste. In a small bowl,
whisk the egg yolk into the cream. Stir in 1/2 cup of the soup and mix
well. Add to the soup, stirring rapidly.
Cook for 2 minutes, being careful that it does not boil.
Serve.

Vermont cheddar
cheese is a white cheddar.
You can substitute any
type of cheddar cheese if
you are unable to find Vermont.

Cheddar Cheese and Pimiento

Yield: 6 servings
Cooking time: 40 minutes

2 teaspoons vegetable oil
1 1/2 cups chopped onions
2 cloves garlic, minced
2 cups peeled and cubed potatoes
1/4 cup drained, canned, diced mild
   green chilies
1/4 cup drained, chopped, bottled
   pimientos

1/4 teaspoon dried thyme
1/2 teaspoon dried cilantro leaves
1/4 teaspoon salt
1/4 teaspoon freshly ground black
   pepper
3 cups chicken broth
1 lb. shredded cheddar cheese

In a 2 quart stock pot, sauté the onions and garlic in the oil over medium heat for 5 minutes. Add the potatoes, chilies, pimientos, thyme, cilantro, salt and pepper. Stir well. Add the chicken broth and bring to a boil. Lower the heat, cover and simmer until the potatoes are tender, about 20 minutes. In a food processor, purée the soup in batches, being careful not to splatter the hot liquid. Return the purée to the stock pot and bring to a boil. Reduce the heat to low and stir in the cheese until it is melted. Serve.

Cheese soup doesn't have to be boring! Chilies and pimientos add color and flavor to this cheddar cheese recipe.

Roquefort

Yield: 6 servings
Cooking time: 60 minutes

1 medium-sized onion
3 celery stalks, including leaves
4 carrots, peeled
3 tablespoons butter
6 cups chicken broth

5 oz. Roquefort cheese
4 tablespoons cream
2 egg yolks
Salt and pepper to taste
1/4 cup finely chopped walnuts
  (optional)

In a food processor, mince the onion, celery, and carrots individually. Melt the butter in a 4 quart stock pot. Add the vegetables and cook over medium heat for 10 minutes. Add the chicken broth, bring to a boil, reduce heat, cover and simmer for 15 minutes. In a small bowl, mash the Roquefort cheese. Blend in the cream and then the egg yolks. Add 1/3 cup of the hot soup. Mix well. Remove the soup from the heat. Stir in the Roquefort cheese mixture. Salt and pepper to taste. Mix well. Serve sprinkled with finely chopped walnuts.

This soup is a great beginning to an elegant meal.

Cream of Brie and Leek

Yield: 8 servings
Cooking time: 60 minutes

1/2 cup unsalted butter
8 large leeks (white part only), finely
    chopped
4 cups unsalted chicken broth
1/2 cup flour
4 cups half and half
1 1/2 lbs. Brie cheese
Salt and freshly ground pepper to taste
Chopped chives garnish

In a heavy 6 quart stock pot, melt 1/4 cup butter. Add the leeks and sauté for 5 minutes. Add the chicken broth and bring to a boil. Reduce the heat and simmer, covered, for 25 minutes. Strain the leeks from the broth. In a food processor, purée the leeks with 1/2 cup of the broth. Pour back into the stock pot and keep the heat on low. Melt the remaining 1/4 cup butter in the microwave or a saucepan. Stir the flour into the butter. Blend to create a smooth paste. Add the paste to the soup stock and stir well. Blend in the half and half, one cup at a time. Whisk until smooth. Chop the brie cheese into small cubes, including the rind. Add the cheese to the soup in small batches, blending until smooth. It will take a little time for the cheese to melt, but do not turn up the heat or the half and half will scald. Stir and blend the cheese until it is all melted. Dip a small strainer into the soup to remove the brie cheese rinds. You may leave the rinds in the soup, if you enjoy their flavor. Season with salt and pepper. Sprinkle with chopped chives. Serve.

The distinctive flavor of brie cheese is showcased in this rich recipe.

Cream of Broccoli

Yield: 4 servings
Cooking time: 40 minutes

4 cups fresh broccoli
1/2 cup chopped onion
1 chicken bouillon cube
1/2 teaspoon Worcestershire sauce
1/4 teaspoon seasoned salt

1/4 teaspoon celery salt
Dash nutmeg
3 cups water
3 teaspoons cornstarch
3/4 cup lowfat milk

Chop the broccoli stems and tops into bite-sized pieces. In a 2 quart stock pot, combine the broccoli, onions, bouillon, Worcestershire sauce, seasoned salt, celery salt, and nutmeg. Add water and bring to a boil. Simmer over medium heat until the vegetables are tender, about 25 minutes. Place the cornstarch into a small bowl. Add 2 tablespoons of the vegetable liquid and stir until smooth. Next stir it into the soup. Add the milk and heat through. Do not boil. Serve.

If you are a broccoli lover, this is a soup for you.

Cream of Cauliflower

Yield: 4 servings
Cooking time: 25 minutes

1 large head of cauliflower
1 medium-sized potato, diced
1 small onion, diced
2 teaspoons salt
1/8 teaspoon ground white pepper
1/2 teaspoon savory
2 cups chicken broth
1 cup half and half

Wash the cauliflower and chop off the flowerets. Place the flowerets, diced potato, diced onion, salt, pepper, savory and chicken broth into a 4 quart stock pot. Stir well. Bring to a boil, lower heat, cover and simmer for 15 minutes. In a food processor, purée the soup in batches, being careful not to splatter the hot liquid. Return the purée to the stock pot. Stir in the half and half. Heat through and serve.

Cream of Mushroom

Yield: 6 servings
Cooking time: 20 minutes

4 tablespoons butter
1 lb. fresh mushrooms, coarsely
    chopped
3 tablespoons chopped onion
1 tablespoon flour
1/2 cup cream sherry
3 cups beef stock
1/4 teaspoon dried thyme

1/2 teaspoon dry mustard
1/4 teaspoon garlic powder
1/4 teaspoon freshly ground
    pepper
1 cup half and half
1/8 teaspoon salt
2 tablespoons fresh parsley

   In a 4 quart stock pot, melt the butter over medium heat. Add the
mushrooms and onion. Cook for 15 minutes until the vegetables are tender. Stir in the flour and the sherry. Cook for 1 minute. Blend the soup in
batches in a food processor until smooth. Be careful not to splatter the hot
liquid. Add 1 cup of the beef stock, thyme, dry mustard, garlic powder,
and pepper and blend until smooth. Pour back into the stock pot and stir
in the remaining broth, half and half, and salt. Heat through, but don't
boil. Ladle into warm soup bowls. Garnish with fresh parsley.

The sherry
adds a sophisti-
cated taste to the
mushrooms in
this recipe.

90

Cream of Spinach

Yield: 4 servings
Cooking time: 20 minutes

20 ounces of fresh spinach
3 tablespoons unsalted butter
3/4 cup chopped onion
1 cup chicken stock
2 cups lowfat milk
1/4 teaspoon salt
1/8 teaspoon ground white pepper

Wash the spinach thoroughly and break off the stems. Do not dry the leaves. Place the spinach in a 6 quart stock pot, with just the water from the rinsing. Cover and cook over high heat for about 10 minutes until wilted. Meanwhile, melt butter in a large skillet and sauté the onions until golden. Drain the spinach, reserving the liquid, and place the spinach in a food processor along with the onions. Purée until smooth. Pour the purée back into the stock pot with the spinach liquid. Add the chicken stock, milk, salt and pepper. Stir and slowly bring to a simmer. Serve.

Cream of Zucchini and Carrot

Yield: 6 servings
Cooking time: 25 minutes

4 cups chicken broth
4 medium-sized zucchini, sliced
2 carrots, sliced
1 onion, chopped

1 (8-oz.) package cream cheese
1/8 teaspoon salt
Dash pepper

Pour the chicken broth into a 2 quart saucepan. Add the zucchini, carrots and onion. Bring to a boil, lower heat, cover and simmer for 20 minutes, until the carrots are tender. Strain the vegetables, reserving the broth. Purée the vegetables in a blender with the softened cream cheese and 1/2 cup of the broth. Be careful not to splatter the hot vegetables. Stir the purée back into the broth. Add salt and pepper. Heat through and serve.

Seafood

Cajun Crab

Yield: 12 servings
Cooking time: 1 hour 20 minutes

1 tablespoon vegetable oil
1 1/3 cups chopped red onion
1 1/3 cups chopped celery
3/4 cup chopped green pepper
3 garlic cloves, minced
1 tablespoon Worcestershire sauce
1/2 teaspoon salt
1/2 teaspoon dried thyme
1/4 teaspoon ground white pepper
4 cups chicken broth
2 cups water
2 (9 oz.) packages frozen shoepeg
    white corn

1 (10-oz.) can diced tomatoes and
    green chilies, undrained
1 (6-oz.) can tomato paste
1 cup chopped green onion
1 lb. fresh lump crabmeat,
    chopped

Heat oil in a 4 quart stock pot. Add the red onion, celery, green
pepper, and garlic. Sauté for 5 minutes, then add the Worcestershire
sauce, salt, thyme, pepper, broth, water, corn, diced tomatoes and green
chilies, and tomato paste. Stir well and bring to a boil. Reduce the heat
and simmer, uncovered, for 1 hour. Stir in the green onions and crabmeat,
and cook over medium heat for 15 minutes. Serve.

This soup has a spicy Cajun taste. If you prefer a less spicy taste, use
a 14.5 oz. can of plain diced tomatoes, instead of the diced tomatoes and
green chilies.

New England Clam Chowder

Yield: 12 servings
Cooking time: 45 minutes

5 large potatoes
3/4 stick butter
2 cups chopped celery
1 cup chopped carrots
1 cup chopped onion
1 teaspoon ground white pepper

1 teaspoon garlic salt
1 cup chicken broth
2 (8 oz.) cans clam juice
1 1/2 cups flour
5 cups 2% milk
4 (6.5 oz.) cans chopped clams

Peel and quarter the potatoes. In a 2 quart saucepan, boil the potatoes in lightly salted water. In a 4 quart stock pot, melt the butter and sauté the celery, carrots, and onion. Stir in the white pepper, garlic salt, chicken bouillon cube and clam juice. Simmer over medium heat for 5 minutes and then bring to a boil. In a medium sized bowl, whisk together the flour and 3 cups milk. Whisk into the stock. Mixture will be thick. Add the remaining 2 cups of milk slowly. Cut the boiled potatoes into bite-sized pieces. Stir in the potatoes and clams. Heat through and serve.

Michelle, my friend, the chef, gave me her chowder recipe that is famous in Cleveland.

Manhattan Clam Chowder

Yield: 10 servings
Cooking time: 60 minutes

5 cups water
1 lb. shrimp
6 small new potatoes, quartered
3 bacon strips, cut into small pieces
1 onion, chopped
2 stalks celery, chopped
1/2 green pepper, chopped
1/4 cup flour
1 (14.5 oz.) can stewed tomatoes
1 1/2 cups tomato purée

1/8-1/4 teaspoon white pepper
1/4 teaspoon salt
1/4 teaspoon parsley flakes
1/4 teaspoon marjoram
1/8-1/4 teaspoon cayenne
  pepper
1/4 teaspoon garlic powder
1/4 teaspoon thyme
1/4 teaspoon dry mustard
2 (10 oz.) can clams, drained
  and chopped

Bring the water to a boil in a 6 quart stock pot. Add the shrimp, lower heat to medium, and cook for 15 minutes. Remove the shrimp, and then peel, devein, and chop them. Set aside. Strain the stock through cheesecloth and set it aside. Place the quartered new potatoes in a medium-sized saucepan. Cover with water and bring to a boil. Cook over high heat for 15 minutes, or until potatoes are tender.

In the meantime, fry the bacon in the stock pot until it is crisp. Remove the bacon and set it aside. Sauté the onion, celery and bell pepper in the bacon drippings for 5 minutes. Stir in the flour. Add the reserved fish stock, stewed tomatoes, tomato purée and all of the seasonings. Stir well. Bring to a boil, reduce heat, cover and simmer for 15 minutes. Add the shrimp, clams, bacon, and potatoes. Simmer, covered, for an additional 15 minutes. Serve.

This recipe epitomizes everything I love in a red clam chowder. I know that you will enjoy it!

Shrimp Bisque

Yield: 12 servings
Cooking time: 45 minutes

2 quarts water
4 1/2 lbs. fresh shrimp
3 bay leaves
1 lemon
1/2 cup butter
6 stalks celery, chopped
1 onion, chopped
1/2 teaspoon paprika

1 teaspoon salt
1/4 teaspoon ground white pepper
1/2 cup flour
1 pint half and half
1/2 cup dry sherry
4 tablespoons tomato paste
1/8 to 1/4 teaspoon hot sauce

Pour the water into a 4 quart stock pot, and bring to a boil. Add the shrimp and bay leaves. Squeeze the juice from the lemon. Add the juice and the lemon halves to the stock pot. Reduce heat and simmer for 20 minutes. Strain the shrimp from the broth, reserving the stock. Then strain the stock through cheesecloth and set it aside. Melt the butter in the stock pot. Add the chopped celery and onion. Sauté for 15 minutes over medium high heat. Add the paprika, salt and pepper. Stir in the flour, a little at a time. Slowly whisk in the reserved fish stock. Stir in the sherry, half and half and tomato paste until well blended. Peel and devein the shrimp. Chop into small pieces. Stir into the soup with the hot sauce. Heat through and serve.

This wonderful shrimp soup is easy to make. Your family or guests will love it!

Seafood Gumbo

Yield: 10 servings
Cooking time: 1 hour 50 minutes

Shrimp Stock:

2 quarts water
1 1/2 lbs. raw medium-sized
   shrimp in shell
2 large onions, quartered, skins
   left on
3 stalks celery, cut in 1 inch pieces
5 bay leaves
1 tablespoon dried thyme
Juice of 2 lemons

   Combine all ingredients in a 6 quart stock pot. Bring water to a boil
and cook 20 minutes, until the onions and celery are transparent. Shrimp
will be somewhat overcooked to extract the most flavor from them. Strain
and reserve the liquid. Remove the shrimp and peel. Chop the shrimp
into small pieces and set aside.

Soup

1/2 cup butter
3 cloves garlic, minced
2 large onions, diced
1 bell pepper, diced
2 stalks celery, diced
Reserved shrimp stock
1 cup flour
2 (14.5 oz.) cans diced tomatoes,
  drained

Cayenne pepper to taste
Salt to taste
1 teaspoon ground thyme
3 teaspoons Gumbo File Powder
1 pint oysters
1/2 lb. flake crabmeat, chopped
  Reserved chopped shrimp

In the 6 quart stock pot, melt the butter. Over medium heat, sauté the garlic, onions, pepper, and celery for 15 minutes. Stir in the flour. Add the shrimp stock, a pint at a time, blending well after each addition. Add the diced tomatoes. Turn heat to low and simmer, uncovered, for 45 minutes, stirring occasionally. In the meantime, place the raw oysters into a large frying pan. Add a little white wine and water or just water to cover. Poach for 8-10 minutes over medium high heat. Drain and chop into bite-sized pieces. Set aside. After 45 minutes, the soup should be thick enough to coat the back of a spoon, if not, simmer another 15 minutes. Add cayenne pepper and salt to taste, the ground thyme and Gumbo File Powder. Stir well. Add the chopped oysters, chopped crab, and shrimp. Stir well and heat through. Serve over white rice.

Serve this recipe as the main course and surprise your guests with your Creole background. They'll never guess that the Gumbo File Powder came from your local supermarket.

Oyster Stew

Yield: 6 servings
Cooking time: 60 minutes

1 clove garlic
5 slices bacon, cut into small pieces
5 carrots, diced
1 medium-sized onion, diced
3 stalks celery, diced
4 tablespoons butter
1 1/2 tablespoons Worcestershire sauce

1 lb. fresh oysters with juice
4 potatoes, peeled and diced
1/4 teaspoon salt
1/4 teaspoon fresh ground pepper
4 cups skim milk
1 (16 oz.) package of frozen corn

Rub the garlic clove around the inside of a 4 quart stock pot. Add the bacon, carrots, onion, and celery. Sauté, stirring often, for 10 minutes, until the bacon is crisp. Melt the butter in a medium-sized saucepan. Add the Worcestershire and oysters with their juice. Stir well. Cook on medium heat for 5 minutes, until the edges of the oysters start to curl. (You may want to cut the oysters in half.) Set aside. Save liquid from oysters.

Add the potatoes to the vegetables with 1 cup of the oyster liquid. Add the salt and pepper. Cook over medium heat for 15 minutes, until the potatoes are tender. In a food processor, purée the vegetables in batches, being careful not to splatter the hot liquid. Return the purée to the stock pot. Stir in the milk. Add the oyster mixture and the corn. Cook over low heat for 30 minutes, stirring often. Be careful not to scald the milk. Serve.

 My sister, Stephanie, shared her special recipe with me.

Shrimp and Asparagus

Yield: 6 servings
Cooking time: 30 minutes

8 cups chicken broth
1 lb. asparagus
1 1/2 cups dried egg noodles
1 lb. large shrimp, peeled and
   deveined
6 green onions, white part only,
   diced

2 eggs
1/2 teaspoon salt
1/8 teaspoon ground white
   pepper
2 teaspoons soy sauce

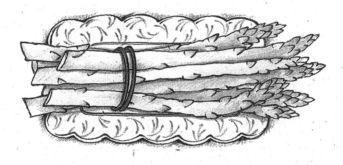

   In a 4 quart stock pot, bring the chicken broth to a boil. Cut the tips off
of the asparagus and set them aside. Cut the asparagus stalks diagonally into 1 inch pieces. Add the asparagus stalks to the chicken broth.
Lower heat to a gentle boil and cook for 10 minutes. Add the egg noodles
and cook for 5 minutes. Add the shrimp and green onions. Cook for 10
minutes. Remove the soup from the heat. In a small bowl, whisk the eggs
with the salt and pepper. Pour the egg mixture steadily into the soup,
stirring constantly so that it remains in shreds. Stir in the soy sauce.
Serve.

Seafood Tortellini

Yield: 8 servings
Cooking time: 30 minutes

1 tablespoon olive oil
1 onion, chopped
1 garlic clove, minced
1/2 red bell pepper, chopped
1/2 green bell pepper, chopped
1 small zucchini, diced
1 tablespoon Herbs de Provence
1/2 teaspoon salt
1/4 teaspoon ground white pepper

5 cups chicken broth
1 1/2 cups dry white wine
1 (13 oz.) package cheese tortellini
1/2 lb. halibut, cut into small pieces
1/2 lb. sea scallops, cut in half crosswise
Juice of 1 lemon
1 (14.5 oz.) can stewed tomatoes

Heat the oil in an 8 quart stock pot. Add the onion, garlic, bell peppers, zucchini, Herbs de Provence, salt and pepper. Sauté for 10 minutes. Add the chicken broth and wine. Bring to a boil. Add the cheese tortellini and cook for 10 minutes at a gentle boil. Add the halibut and sea scallops and cook for 5 minutes. Stir in the lemon juice and stewed tomatoes. Cook for 5 minutes more and serve.

20 Minute Soups

Asparagus and Escarole

Yield: 6 servings
Cooking time: 20 minutes

2 tablespoons olive oil
1 lb. thin asparagus, sliced
   diagonally into 1/2 inch pieces
3 scallions, minced
6 cups chicken broth
1/2 teaspoon ground thyme

1/2 teaspoon garlic salt
1/8 teaspoon ground white pepper
4 cups loosely packed, chopped
   escarole leaves
8 fresh basil leaves, chopped

Heat the oil in a 4 quart stock pot. Add the asparagus and scallions and sauté for 10 minutes over medium heat. Add the chicken broth and bring to a boil. Stir in the ground thyme, garlic salt and pepper. Add the escarole leaves, and basil leaves.

Lower heat and simmer for 10 minutes. Serve.

Asparagus and escarole combine flavors in this easy recipe.

Black Bean and Pinto Chili

Yield: 6 servings
Cooking time: 20 minutes

1 lb. ground beef
1/2 cup chopped onion
1/4 teaspoon garlic powder
1 (15 oz.) can black beans
1 (15 oz.) can pinto beans
1 (28 oz.) can diced tomatoes

1 (6 oz.) can tomato paste
1 1/3 cups water
1 1/2 teaspoons salt
1/4 teaspoon ground black pepper
1 teaspoon chili powder

In a large saucepan, brown the ground beef with the chopped onion. Stir in the remaining ingredients. Cook for 15 minutes. Serve topped with cheddar cheese and sour cream.

This is a terrific quick chili! Black beans and pinto beans create a rich flavor.

Bean and Bacon Chowder

Yield: 6 servings
Cooking time: 20 minutes

6 slices bacon, chopped
1 small onion, chopped
1/2 medium-sized green pepper,
  seeded and chopped
1/2 lb. frankfurters, sliced
1 teaspoon chili powder
1 celery stalk, sliced
1 (13.75 oz.) can beef broth

1 (15 oz.) can Great Northern beans,
  drained
1 (16 oz.) can stewed tomatoes
1 (15. oz.) can small whole potatoes,
  drained
1 teaspoon salt
1/4 teaspoon black pepper

In a 4 quart stock pot, sauté the bacon until it is crisp. Remove and drain it on paper towels. Set aside. Sauté the onion, green pepper, frankfurters, and chili powder in the bacon drippings for 8 minutes. Stir frequently. Add the celery, beef broth and Great Northern beans. Stir well and bring to a boil. In a food processor, purée the stewed tomatoes, with their liquid, and the potatoes. Add the purée to the soup with the salt and pepper. Stir well, reduce heat, cover and simmer for 5 minutes. Add the bacon and serve.

It's hard to believe that the hearty flavors in this recipe can happen so quickly.

Bouillabaisse

Yield: *6 servings*
Cooking time: *20 minutes*

1 tablespoon vegetable oil
1 cup sliced onions
2 stalks celery, sliced diagonally
2 cloves garlic, minced
4 cups chicken broth
1 (28 oz.) can crushed tomatoes
1 (6.5 oz.) can minced clams
   with juice
1/2 cup dry white wine
1 teaspoon Worcestershire sauce
1/2 teaspoon dried basil leaves
1/4 teaspoon crushed red pepper
1 bay leaf
1 cup cooked shrimp
1 cup crabmeat, chopped

Pour the oil into a 6 quart stock pot. Add the onions, celery and garlic. Sauté for 3 minutes. Stir in the chicken broth, crushed tomatoes, clams with juice, wine, Worcestershire, basil, red pepper, and bay leaf. Bring to a boil. Reduce heat to low and simmer for 15 minutes. Stir in shrimp and crabmeat and heat through. Serve.

Your guests will think that you worked for hours making this soup!

Cheddar Cheese Chive

Yield: 4 servings
Cooking time: 20 minutes

1 (14.5 oz.) can vegetable broth
1 teaspoon dried minced onion
1/4 teaspoon minced garlic

2 teaspoons chopped chives
2 cups grated cheddar cheese
1/2 cup milk

Pour the vegetable broth into a medium-sized saucepan. Add the minced onion, garlic and chives. Bring to a boil. Add the cheddar cheese and stir well as it melts. Lower heat and add the milk. Stir constantly until heated through. Serve.

This very simple cheese soup is a nice start to your meal.

Chicken Gnocchi

Yield: 6 servings
Cooking time: 20 minutes

8 cups chicken broth
1/2 teaspoon minced onion
1 lb. package of gnocchi
2 carrots, shredded
1 cup diced, cooked chicken

1/4 teaspoon ground oregano
1/8 teaspoon ground white pepper
1/3 cup chopped fresh parsley
Parmesan cheese (optional)

In a 4 quart stock pot, bring the chicken broth and minced onion to a boil. Add the gnocchi and cook for 5 minutes. Add the carrots, chicken, oregano, pepper, and parsley. Stir well. Simmer for 10 minutes. Serve garnished with Parmesan cheese.

The rich flavor of chicken broth showcases gnocchi in this recipe.

Crab Bisque

Yield: 6 servings
Cooking time: 20 minutes

1/4 cup butter
1/4 cup celery, minced
3 scallions, minced
1/4 cup flour

2 tablespoons shrimp cocktail sauce
4 cups skim milk
16 oz. fresh crabmeat (3 1/2 cups)

In a large saucepan, melt the butter. Add the celery and scallions and sauté for 5 minutes. Add the flour and cocktail sauce. Mix well. Raise heat to medium high, and gradually add the milk, stirring constantly. When the milk begins to boil, reduce heat and simmer. Add the crabmeat and cook for 3 minutes, until crab is hot. Serve.

Seafood soups are easy to make-- and so flavorful.

Hamburger

Yield: 6 servings
Cooking time: 20 minutes

1 1/2 lbs. ground beef
3 cups water
1 package onion soup mix
1 (28 oz.) can whole tomatoes, chopped
1 (12 oz.) can tomato paste
3 teaspoons salt

1 teaspoon black pepper
1/2 teaspoon garlic powder
1 (16 oz.) package frozen mixed vegetables
2 tablespoons parsley flakes
1 tablespoon Worcestershire sauce

In a 6 quart stock pot, brown the ground beef. Pour off the excess grease. Stir in the water and onion soup mix. Add the undrained, chopped tomatoes, tomato paste, salt, pepper and garlic powder. Bring to a boil, lower heat, cover and simmer for 10 minutes. Add the frozen vegetables, parsley flakes and Worcestershire sauce. Cover and cook for 10 minutes. Serve.

Take the hamburger out of the bun and put it into this easy soup recipe!

Italian Cream of Tomato

This is more than an easy delicious tomato soup recipe! It is outstanding!

Yield: 6 servings
Cooking time: 20 minutes

2 cups chicken broth
1 small onion, chopped
2 tablespoons chopped green pepper
1 tablespoon chopped celery
1/2 teaspoon garlic powder
1/4 teaspoon ground white pepper

1 (16 oz.) can Italian stewed tomatoes
1 (8 oz.) can tomato sauce
1 (6 oz.) can tomato paste
1 tablespoon sugar
1 cup half-and-half

In a large saucepan, combine the chicken broth and the onion, green pepper, celery, garlic, and pepper. Bring to a boil. Reduce heat and simmer, uncovered, for 5 minutes or until the vegetables are tender. Add the undrained stewed tomatoes, tomato sauce, tomato paste and sugar. Bring the mixture to a boil. Reduce the heat and simmer, uncovered, for 15 minutes. Stir in the half-and-half. Heat through and serve.

Lobster Bisque

Yield: 4 servings
Cooking time: 20 minutes

1 (10 oz.) can condensed
   tomato soup
1 (10 oz.) can cream of celery
   soup
1 cup cream
1 cup milk
1 lb. fresh lobster meat
2 tablespoons cream sherry

In a large saucepan, stir together the tomato soup, cream of celery soup, cream and milk. Cook over medium heat for 15 minutes until soup is hot. Whisk several times to make it smooth. Add the lobster meat and cook for 5 minutes, until heated through. Stir in the sherry and serve.

Another seafood soup recipe that will fool your guests into thinking you spent all day cooking.

Potato Corn Chowder

Yield: 6 servings
Cooking time: 20 minutes

2 (14.5 oz.) cans chicken broth
1/2 cup chopped onion
1/2 cup chopped carrots
1/8 teaspoon ground thyme
2 (15 oz.) cans whole potatoes
2 (15 oz.) cans whole kernel corn

1/2 cup half and half
1 teaspoon salt
1/8 teaspoon ground white pepper
Optional: 1 cup julienne cut smoked
    ham
Parsley flakes

Pour the chicken broth into a 4 quart stock pot. Add the onion, carrots and thyme and bring to a boil. Reduce the heat and simmer for 10 minutes. Drain the potatoes and chop one cup full. Set aside. Place the remaining potatoes in a food processor. Drain the cans of corn. Set one can aside. Add the other can of corn to the food processor. Add two cups of the chicken broth. Purée until smooth, being careful not to splatter the hot liquid. Stir the purée into the stock pot. Add the diced potatoes, the rest of the corn, the half and half, salt, pepper and ham. Bring to a boil, reduce heat and simmer for 5 minutes. Serve garnished with parsley flakes.

This recipe warms you up fast on a cold winter evening.

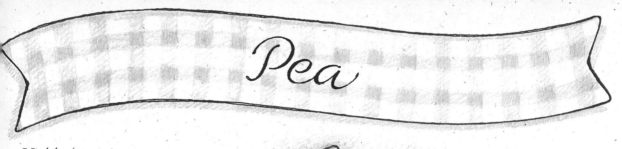

Pea

Yield: *6 servings*
Cooking time: *20 minutes*

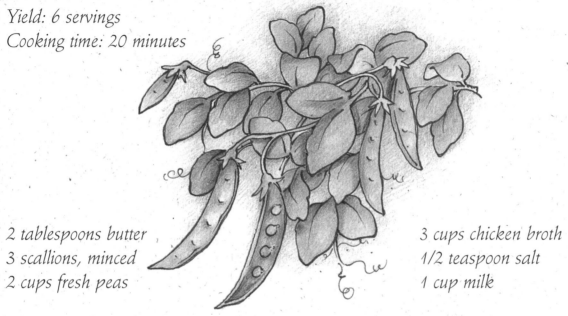

2 tablespoons butter
3 scallions, minced
2 cups fresh peas

3 cups chicken broth
1/2 teaspoon salt
1 cup milk

In a 2 quart saucepan, sauté the scallions in the butter for 2 minutes. Add the peas and coat them with the butter. Add the chicken broth and salt and bring to a boil. Lower heat and simmer, covered, for 15 minutes. In a food processor, purée the mixture in batches, being careful not to splatter the hot liquid. Return the purée to the saucepan. Add the milk and cook over medium high heat, stirring constantly, until the soup is heated through. Serve.

When you don't want to soak dried peas overnight, this recipe fills the bill for a fast, terrific pea soup.

Salmon and Corn Chowder

Yield: 6 servings
Cooking time: 20 minutes

2 tablespoons olive oil
2/3 cup chopped onion
1/2 cup chopped celery
1 cup unpeeled red potatoes, diced
1/2 cup water
1 lb. salmon steaks
1/4 cup flour
4 cups low-fat milk
2 ears fresh corn, shucked and cut off
  the cob
1/8 teaspoon freshly ground white
  pepper
1/2 teaspoon salt
1 1/2 cups white wine
10 dashes Tabasco™ sauce
3 teaspoons white wine Worcestershire

In a large saucepan, sauté the onion and celery in the olive oil. Add the diced potatoes and water. Bring to a boil, cover, and cook over medium heat for 10 minutes until the potatoes are tender.

Pour the white wine into a large skillet. Add the salmon steaks, cover, and poach over medium-high heat for 10 minutes until the salmon is cooked through. Set aside.

In a small bowl, whisk the flour with 1/4 cup of the milk to make a paste. Slowly stir the paste into the potato mixture. Stir in the rest of the milk. Add the corn, pepper, and salt. Bring to a gentle boil. Cut the salmon steaks into bite-sized chunks. Add to the soup with the Tabasco™ and white wine Worcestershire. Stir well, simmer for 5 minutes until the salmon is heated through. Serve.

Salmon lends a nice flavor to this creamy corn chowder.

Vegetable Cheese

Yield: 4 servings
Cooking time: 20 minutes

2 teaspoons vegetable oil
1/4 cup chopped red pepper
1/4 cup chopped onion
2 tablespoons flour
1/2 teaspoon dry mustard

1/2 teaspoon salt
2 cups skim milk
1 (10 oz.) package frozen country
    blend vegetables, thawed
2 cups shredded cheddar cheese

In a large saucepan, heat the oil. Add the red pepper and onion. Sauté for 5 minutes. Remove from heat. Stir in the flour, dry mustard, and salt. Return to medium high heat, add the milk, and cook until it comes to a gentle boil. Stir often, being careful not to scald the milk. Add the vegetables and the cheese. Cook, stirring frequently, for 15 minutes until the cheese melts. Serve.

Substitute your favorite frozen vegetables or favorite cheese in this recipe.

Leftovers

Baked Bean

Yield: 6 servings
Cooking time: 40 minutes

2 tablespoons olive oil
1 cup onion, finely chopped
1 garlic clove, minced
1 celery stalk, finely chopped
1 tablespoon whole wheat flour

2 cups leftover baked beans
1 (13.75 oz.) can beef broth
1 (14.5 oz.) can diced tomatoes
1/4 cup hickory barbecue sauce
1 teaspoon Worcestershire sauce

Heat the oil in a 3 quart stock pot. Add the onion, garlic, and celery and sauté 5 minutes, stirring constantly. Stir in the flour. Add the baked beans, beef broth, diced tomatoes, barbecue sauce, and Worcestershire sauce. Bring to a boil, lower heat, cover, and simmer for 30 minutes. Stir occasionally. Serve.

If you love baked beans like I do, why not put them in a soup?

Chicken and Broccoli

Yield: 4 servings
Cooking time: 20 minutes

2 tablespoons olive oil
3 tablespoons minced onion
1 stalk celery, minced
3 tablespoons flour
1/4 teaspoon salt
2 cups milk
1 cup chicken broth
1 1/2 cups chopped cooked chicken
2 cups chopped cooked broccoli
1/4 teaspoon allspice

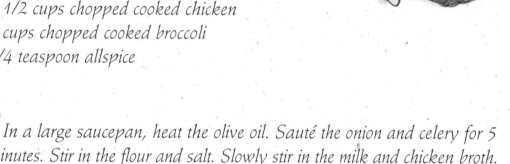

In a large saucepan, heat the olive oil. Sauté the onion and celery for 5 minutes. Stir in the flour and salt. Slowly stir in the milk and chicken broth. Cook over medium heat, stirring often until the broth begins to boil. Add the chopped chicken, broccoli and allspice. Stir well. Heat through and serve.

Use up your leftover "tree tops" in this recipe.

Chicken Tortellini

Yield: 6 servings
Cooking time: 20 minutes

8 cups chicken broth
1 (9 oz.) package cheese tortellini
1 (10 oz.) package frozen
  chopped spinach
1 teaspoon basil

1/8 teaspoon ground white pepper
1/2 teaspoon minced onion
1 1/2 cups diced, cooked chicken
1/4 cup chopped fresh parsley

In a 4 quart stock pot, bring the chicken broth to a boil. Add the tortellini and cook for 10 minutes over medium high heat. Add the chopped spinach, basil, ground white pepper, minced onion, and chicken and cook for 10 minutes over medium high heat. Serve garnished with fresh parsley.

Where's the tortellini? Hiding behind the chopped spinach, of course.

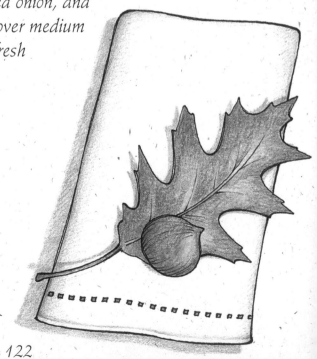

Cream of Chicken with Rice

Yield: 4 servings
Cooking time: 25 minutes

4 cups chicken broth
1/4 teaspoon minced garlic
2 stalks celery, minced
1 1/2 cups cooked chicken or
 turkey, finely diced
1 (15 oz.) can cream-style
 sweet corn
1 1/2 cups cooked rice
3/4 cup half and half
1/2 teaspoon salt

Bring the chicken broth to a
boil in a 4 quart stock pot.
Add the garlic and celery. Lower
heat and cook for 10 minutes. Add the
chicken, cream-style corn, and rice. Cook for 10 minutes over medium-
high heat. Stir in the half and half and salt. Cook for 5 minutes, until
heated through. Serve.

🍃 Cream of chicken soup fast. I love it!

Hot and Sour

Yield: 6 servings
Cooking time: 30 minutes

6 scallions
8 cups chicken broth
1 2-inch-long piece fresh ginger,
   peeled and thinly sliced
1/2 teaspoon ground white pepper
2 teaspoons vegetable oil
1/4 lb. fresh shiitake mushrooms, stems
   removed, thinly sliced

4 cups chopped Napa cabbage
2 cups cooked dark turkey or chicken
   meat, diced
2 tablespoons cornstarch
1/4 cup rice-wine vinegar
1 large egg, lightly beaten

Remove the green portions of the scallions, thinly slice and set aside. Cut the white portions into 2-inch lengths. Place the scallion whites, chicken broth, ginger, and white pepper into a 2 quart stock pot. Bring to a boil, reduce heat, and simmer for 15 minutes. Strain through a sieve and reserve the stock. Rinse and dry the sauce pan; add oil and heat on high. Add mushrooms and sauté until they start to soften, about 1 minute. Add the cabbage and sauté for one more minute. Add the reserved stock and simmer for 5 minutes. Reduce heat to low and simmer for 10 minutes. Add the turkey or chicken meat and simmer for 5 minutes. In a small bowl, dissolve the cornstarch in the vinegar. Add to the soup and stir until thickened, about 1 minute. Remove the soup from the heat. Slowly pour in the beaten egg, stirring constantly so that it remains in shreds. Serve garnished with the scallion greens.

Reuben Chowder

Yield: 4 servings
Cooking time: 20 minutes

1 (14.5 oz.) can beef broth
2 (14.5 oz.) cans vegetable broth
1 tablespoon olive oil
1/2 of a medium-sized onion, sliced
1/2 teaspoon celery salt
1/2 teaspoon ground mustard
1 teaspoon Worcestershire sauce

2-3 teaspoons stoneground horseradish
  mustard
1 cup cooked corned beef, sliced
1 cup sauerkraut
4 slices of Swiss cheese, cut into thin
  slices
Horseradish to taste

   Bring the beef and vegetable broths to a boil in a 4 quart stock pot. In the meantime, heat the olive oil in a small frying pan. Sauté the sliced onions over medium-
high heat for 10 minutes or until browned. Set aside. Stir the celery salt, ground
mustard, Worcestershire sauce and horseradish mustard into the broth. Add the
sliced onions, corned beef and sauerkraut. Reduce heat to low, cover and simmer
for 10 minutes. Serve topped with the Swiss cheese and a dollop of horseradish.

Break out of the sandwich routine
and into the soup!

Spaghetti and Meatballs

Yield: 2 servings
Cooking time: 15 minutes

2 cups cooked spaghetti
2 meatballs, quartered
1 cup beef broth
1 cup tomato juice or tomato
   sauce
1 tablespoon parsley flakes
Parmesan cheese garnish

Optional ingredients:

1 tablespoon minced onion
1/2 teaspoon garlic salt
Chopped fresh vegetables

In a large saucepan, place all of the ingredients. Stir well. Cover and cook for 15 minutes until heated through. Serve garnished with Parmesan cheese.

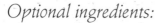 This recipe can be doubled depending on the amount of leftovers. Just keep the proportion of the spaghetti to the liquid even. A great way to use up leftovers!

Swiss Potato

Yield: 4 servings
Cooking time: 15 minutes

2 tablespoons butter
1/4 cup minced onion
2 cups mashed potatoes
2 cups milk

2 cups grated Swiss cheese
1/2 teaspoon salt
Dash pepper

Melt the butter in a 4 quart stock pot. Add the onion and sauté for 8 minutes. Add the mashed potatoes and milk. Blend well. Stir in the Swiss cheese, salt and pepper. Cook until the cheese melts. Serve.

This recipe is great for leftover mashed potatoes. You may substitute with prepared instant mashed potatoes.

Ham and Vegetables

Yield: 4 servings
Cooking time: 25 minutes

1 medium onion, diced
2 stalks celery, diced
2 carrots, sliced
2 (14.5 oz.) cans vegetable
   broth
2 cups diced, cooked ham
1 (14.5 oz) can diced
   tomatoes
1 teaspoon ground mustard
1/4 teaspoon ground white
   pepper
1 cup corn

In a 2 quart stock pot, combine the onion, celery, carrots, vegetable broth, ham, tomatoes, ground mustard and white pepper. Bring to a boil, lower heat, cover and simmer for 20 minutes, until the carrots are tender. Stir in corn and cook until heated through. Serve.

If you're tired of eating leftover ham in a sandwich, try it in soup.

Turkey Dinner

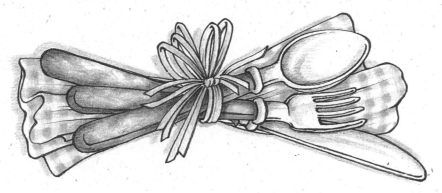

Yield: 4 servings
Cooking time: 15 minutes

2 cups turkey or chicken broth
2 cups leftover vegetables:
  cauliflower, broccoli, carrots, peas
1 teaspoon dill weed
1/2 teaspoon celery salt
1 teaspoon salt
2 cups leftover white turkey meat

1 cup mashed potatoes
1/2 cup plus 2 tablespoons skim
  or whole milk
2 tablespoons flour
4 tablespoons cooked whole
  cranberries (optional)

   Pour the broth into a medium-sized saucepan. Add the vegetables, dill weed, celery salt, and salt. Cook the vegetables for 10 minutes until they are heated up. Add the turkey and potatoes. Pour 1/2 cup milk into the soup and heat through. Put the 2 tablespoons of flour into a small bowl and whisk in the 2 tablespoons milk. Pour into the soup and stir well. Serve immediately. Top with a tablespoon cooked whole cranberries.

Turkey dinner in a bowl!

Turkey Noodle

Yield: 4 servings
Cooking time: 15 minutes

4 cups chicken broth
1 teaspoon minced onion
1/4 teaspoon minced garlic
1 1/2 cups cooked turkey, diced
1 cup frozen or leftover peas

1/2 teaspoon celery salt
Dash ground white pepper
2 tablespoons diced pimientos
1 1/2 cups cooked egg noodles

Bring the chicken broth to a boil in a 4 quart stock pot. Add the onion, garlic, turkey, peas, celery salt, pepper and pimientos. Lower heat, cover and simmer for 10 minutes. Add the cooked noodles and simmer for 5 minutes. Serve.

Around the World

Chinese Sizzling Rice

I was served this wonderfully light soup at a Chinese restaurant, and returned many times to learn the secret of the sizzling rice. The soup is simple to make, has a light taste and the sizzling rice adds a new dimension. You might need to experiment to do the rice just right, but keep on trying.

Yield: 8 servings
Cooking time: 1 hour 5 minutes

Rice:
1 cup long grain rice
2 1/4 cups water
1/2 teaspoon salt
1 1/2 cups vegetable oil

Soup:
10 cups chicken broth
1 stalk celery
1/4 lb. pea pods
1/2 cup shitake mushrooms
3 stalks bok choy
1/2 cup bean sprouts
1/2 cup bamboo shoots
1/2 lb. large shrimp
1 large boneless, skinless,
  chicken breast
Salt and pepper to taste

Rice:

The goal in making this rice is to overcook it so that the rice is browned on the bottom of the pan. Instead of using a saucepan, you may want to use a fry pan that has a lid. Pour the water into your pan and bring it to a boil. Stir in the rice and salt. Reduce heat, cover and simmer over medium low heat for 40 to 50 minutes, until there is a layer of brown rice on the bottom of the pan. Carefully remove the soft, white rice from the top, leaving the layer of browned rice on the bottom. Let the browned rice stand uncovered while you prepare the soup.

Soup:

Pour the chicken broth into an 8 quart stock pot. Bring it to a boil as you prepare the ingredients. Place all of the ingredients into a large bowl as you prepare them. Cut the celery diagonally into thin slices. Remove the tops of the pea pods and then thinly slice them horizontally. Thinly slice the mushrooms. Discard the white stems of the bok choy. Chop up the green leaves. Drain the bean sprouts and bamboo shoots. Peel and devein the shrimp. Butterfly the shrimp by slitting it open along the outside curve. Dice the chicken. Place all of the ingredients into the chicken broth. Lower heat and simmer for 10 minutes.

Sizzling rice:

Pour the vegetable oil into a deep fryer or deep saucepan and turn your heat to high. Scrape the browned rice from the bottom of the pan. It will break into small pieces as you do this. When the oil is hot, drop the rice pieces into it and deep fry for 2 to 3 minutes. Be careful that the oil does not splatter you. If there are any white rice kernels on the brown rice, the moisture could cause the oil to splatter. Quickly fry the rice and place it into a bowl.

Pour the soup into a large soup tureen. Bring it to the table with the fried rice. Pour the fried rice into the soup tureen and you will hear it sizzling. Serve. Salt and pepper to each individual's taste.

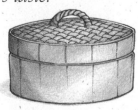

Borscht

Yield: 8 servings
Cooking time: 2 hours 10 minutes

2 medium-sized carrots
6 medium-sized fresh beets
1 celery stalk
1 parsley root
2 leeks, white part only
3 tablespoons butter
2 quarts water
1 1/2 lbs. beef brisket, cut into several
  large chunks

6 whole peppercorns
1 bay leaf
3 teaspoons salt
1 teaspoon freshly ground pepper
2 cups shredded cabbage
1 teaspoon vinegar
Sour cream (optional)

Peel the carrots and 4 of the beets and cut into julienne strips. Slice the celery, parsley root and leeks. In a 6 quart stock pot, melt the butter. Add the vegetables and cook over medium high heat for 5 minutes. Add the water, beef, peppercorns, bay leaf, salt and pepper. Bring to a boil, cover, reduce heat and simmer for 2 hours. In the meantime, grate the other 2 beets. Wrap them in cheesecloth and squeeze the juice into a small bowl. Stir in the vinegar. Set aside. Remove the meat from the stock pot. Slice it and place it into a soup tureen. Add the shredded cabbage to the soup with the vinegar mixture. Cook for 5 minutes. Pour the soup over the meat into the soup tureen. Serve topped with sour cream.

This traditional Russian soup is for beet lovers!

Cioppino

Yield: 8 servings
Cooking time: 1 hour 20 minutes

18 Littleneck clams, scrubbed
2 teaspoons olive oil
1 medium onion, chopped
1 green pepper, chopped
2 garlic cloves, crushed
1/3 cup fresh basil, chopped
1/4 cup celery leaves, finely chopped
2 tablespoons chopped parsley
1/2 teaspoon salt
1 (28 oz.) can crushed plum
  tomatoes
1 1/4 cups Chianti wine
1 tablespoon Worcestershire sauce

1/4 teaspoon hot sauce
1 lb. cod or haddock fillets, cut into 1
  inch chunks
1/2 lb. shrimp, peeled and deveined

Place clams into a 5 quart stock pot. Add water to cover. Bring to a boil, cover,
reduce heat and simmer for 5 minutes, or until clams open. Remove clams and discard empty half of shell. Strain the clam stock through cheesecloth. Set aside.
In the stock pot, heat the oil. Add the onion, green pepper, and garlic. Sauté for 3
minutes. Stir in the basil, salt, celery leaves, parsley, and 1 cup of the reserved
clam stock. Add the tomatoes, wine, Worcestershire sauce, and hot sauce. Bring to
a boil, lower heat and simmer, covered for 1 hour. Add the haddock and shrimp.
Bring to a boil and simmer for 8 minutes, until the fish is firm and the shrimp pink.
Add the clams in the half shell. Heat through and serve.

This Italian seafood soup becomes a hearty meal served with Italian bread
and red wine.

French Onion

Yield: 6 servings
Cooking time: 1 hour 25 minutes

6 large yellow onions, sliced
  very thin
4 tablespoons of butter
1 teaspoon salt
2 teaspoons sugar
2 tablespoons flour
1 1/2 quarts beef stock
4 tablespoons Fino sherry
  or any extra-dry sherry
6 slices of Italian bread
3/4 lb. of Gruyere™ cheese

In a 4 quart stock pot, melt the butter. Stir in the sliced onions. Cover and cook over low heat for 40 minutes until the onions are cooked, but not browned. Stir every 10 minutes or so. Remove the cover, and stir in the salt and sugar. Cook over medium heat, stirring often, for 30 minutes, until the onions are browned. Stir in the flour during the last 5 minutes. In another pan, bring the beef stock to a boil. Add to the onions with the sherry. Bring back to a boil and simmer for 10 minutes. Ladle the soup into individual ovenproof bowls. Top with a slice of bread and a layer of cheese. Place the bowls on a cooking sheet and put under the broiler for 5 minutes, until the cheese is melted and begins to brown. Serve.

You can duplicate the rich French Onion soup you are served at restaurants with this easy recipe.

German Sauerkraut

Yield: 8 servings
Cooking time: 60 minutes

6 slices of smoked bacon
1 medium onion, chopped
1 (14 oz.) can of sauerkraut
1 teaspoon salt
1/2 teaspoon ground black pepper

1/4 teaspoon dried thyme
1 teaspoon caraway seeds
2 cups Riesling wine
4 cups peeled and diced red potatoes
1 quart chicken stock

In a 6 quart stock pot, fry the bacon until it is crisp. Remove and set aside. Drain all but 1 tablespoon of the bacon fat from the stock pot. Sauté the chopped onion in the stock pot until it is slightly browned. Add the sauerkraut, including any juice, salt, black pepper, thyme, caraway seeds and wine. Bring to a boil as you dice the red potatoes. Add the potatoes and chicken stock and bring to a boil once again. Cover and cook over medium heat for 1 hour, until the potatoes are soft. Crumble the bacon and stir into the soup. Serve.

Hungarian Goulash

Yield: 10 servings
Cooking time: 1 hour 40 minutes

2 large onions, coarsely chopped
4 tablespoons butter
1 tablespoon paprika
2 tablespoons cider vinegar
2 lbs. beef shank (cross cut)
10 cups water
1 teaspoon caraway seeds

1/4 teaspoon marjoram leaves
4 beef bouillon cubes
2 teaspoons salt
2 1/2 teaspoons ground pepper
3 medium-sized potatoes, peeled and chopped
2 cups egg noodles

In a 6 quart stock pot, sauté the onions in the butter over medium high heat for 5 minutes, stirring often. Add the paprika, cider vinegar, 8 cups water, caraway seeds and marjoram. Stir well. Bring to a boil. Add the beef shanks, lower heat, cover and cook for 1 hour. Remove the beef from the pot, then remove the meat from the bones. Remove any bones from the stock pot. Cut the meat into bite-sized pieces and return it to the pot. Add the remaining two cups of water. Stir in the bouillon cubes, salt, and pepper and bring to a boil. Add the potatoes and reduce heat, cover and simmer for 20 minutes. Add the egg noodles and cook for 15 minutes. Serve.

 Serve with thick, crusty bread and this soup makes a hearty meal!

Middle Eastern Lamb

Yield: 8 servings
Cooking time: 2 hours 40 minutes

1 1/4 cups dried chickpeas
2 tablespoons olive oil
2 lbs. boneless lamb for stew
1 cup chopped onion
1 cup chopped carrots
1 clove garlic, finely chopped
1/2 teaspoon ground coriander
1/2 teaspoon ground cumin
1/4 teaspoon cayenne pepper
2 (13 3/4 oz.) cans beef broth
1 cup water

1 (28 oz.) can Italian style tomatoes,
  chopped
1 lemon, quartered
Chopped fresh parsley garnish

The night before, place the chickpeas into a medium-sized bowl. Cover with water and soak overnight. The next day, drain the water and set the chickpeas aside. In a 6 quart stock pot, heat the oil over medium heat. Add the lamb and season with salt and pepper. Sauté the lamb, turning so that all sides are browned, for about 10 minutes. Remove the lamb and set it aside. Pour off all but 2 tablespoons of fat. Add the onion, carrots, and garlic. Sauté over medium heat until the onion is translucent, 2-3 minutes. Add the coriander, cumin and cayenne pepper. Sauté for 1 minute more. Pour in the beef broth, water, and chopped Italian tomatoes, with the liquid. Add the lamb, chickpeas and lemon quarters. Bring to a boil, reduce heat and simmer, covered, for 2 1/2 hours. Remove the lemon quarters. Serve garnished with fresh parsley.

Lamb stew--a recipe from Armenia.

Minestrone

Yield: 10 servings
Cooking time: 1 hour 10 minutes

1 (28 oz.) can Italian style tomatoes
2 bay leaves
1/4 teaspoon garlic powder
1 teaspoon ground or dried oregano
2 teaspoons dried parsley
1/2 teaspoon dried basil

1/2 teaspoon salt
1/4 teaspoon ground black pepper
1 cup chopped zucchini
1 cup chopped green beans
1 small onion, chopped
1 cup chopped celery
1 cup chopped carrots
1 (8 oz.) can tomato paste
7 cups beef broth
1 cup medium shell pasta
1 (15 oz.) can dark red kidney
  beans
1 (16 oz.) can large sweet peas
2 tablespoons grated Parmesan
  cheese

This hearty minestrone recipe
will become a family favorite! It
is very easy to make and
very delicious!

Pour the Italian style tomatoes into a 6 quart stock pot. Chop the tomatoes into bite-sized pieces. Add the bay leaves, garlic powder, oregano, dried parsley, dried basil, salt and ground pepper and cook over medium heat. Chop the zucchini and add to the stock pot. Chop the remaining vegetables and add to the stock pot. Stir in the tomato paste. Add the beef broth and bring to a boil. Reduce the heat and simmer for 1/2 hour. While the soup is simmering, in a medium saucepan, bring 1 1/2 quarts of water to a boil. Add pasta shells. Return water to a boil and cook for 10 to 12 minutes, stirring frequently. Drain and set aside.

Drain and rinse the kidney beans and peas. Add to the soup and simmer for 1/2 hour. Add the cooked pasta and Parmesan cheese. Cook until the pasta is heated, about 10 minutes. Remove the bay leaves and serve.

Pasta e Fagioli

Yield: 12 servings
Cooking time: 2 hours

1 1/2 cups dried Northern beans
1 ham hock
1 cup chopped onion
1 cup chopped celery
1 cup chopped carrot
6 cups water
3 cups chicken broth
1 (28 oz.) can plum tomatoes, chopped
1 teaspoon salt
1 teaspoon fennel
1 teaspoon freshly ground black pepper
1 teaspoon oregano
1 1/2 teaspoons sweet pepper flakes
8 oz. short pasta, such as Ziti
3 tablespoons tomato paste
Parmesan cheese

The night before, soak beans in a large bowl in water to cover. The next day, drain the beans. Place in a 6 quart stock pot. Add the 6 cups water and the ham hock. Bring to a boil. In the meantime, chop the onion, celery and carrot. Add to the beans: Cover, turn heat to low and simmer for 1 1/2 hours, until beans are tender. Remove the ham hock and chop the meat into small pieces. Return the meat to the soup. Add the chicken broth and chopped plum tomatoes. Bring to a boil. Stir in the salt, fennel, ground pepper, oregano and sweet pepper flakes. Add the pasta. Reduce heat to medium high and cook the pasta until tender, about 10 minutes. Stir in the tomato paste. Serve topped with Parmesan cheese.

This soup makes a wonderful first course for your Italian meal! Or serve it as the main course!

142

Soupe Au Pistou

Yield: 10 servings
Cooking time: 45 minutes

2 quarts water
2 medium potatoes, pared and sliced
1 cup chopped onion
1 cup sliced carrots
1 cup sliced celery
1 tablespoon salt
1/4 teaspoon ground black pepper

1 1/2 cups fresh green beans, cut
  into 1 inch pieces
1 cup frozen peas
1 cup broken spaghetti
1/2 teaspoon minced garlic
2 tablespoons parsley flakes
2 teaspoons dried basil leaves
1/2 cup grated Parmesan

In a 4 quart stock pot, bring the water to a boil. Add the potatoes, onion, carrots, celery, salt and pepper. Reduce heat, cover and simmer for 30 minutes. Add the fresh green beans, frozen peas and spaghetti. Cook over medium-high heat for 15 minutes or until spaghetti is tender.

While the soup cooks, prepare the pistou. In a blender, process the minced garlic, parsley flakes, dried basil, Parmesan cheese and olive oil to make a smooth paste. Thin with 1/2 cup of the soup broth. Stir the pistou into the soup until well blended. Serve.

This French soup is one of my favorites.

Tortilla Soup

Yield: 6 servings
Cooking time: 35 minutes

1 jalapeno pepper, seeded and
  chopped
1 large onion, chopped
1 tablespoon vegetable oil
1/2 teaspoon minced garlic
1 (14.5 oz.) can tomato purée

4 cups chicken broth
1/2 teaspoon ground cumin
1/8 teaspoon cayenne pepper
2 teaspoons Worcestershire sauce
10 corn tortillas

In a food processor, purée the pepper and onion. Heat the oil in a 4 quart stock pot. Add the pepper and onion purée, and the minced garlic. Sauté for 5 minutes. Add the tomato purée, chicken broth, ground cumin, pepper and Worcestershire sauce. Bring to a boil. Chop the tortillas into small strips. Add to the soup. Turn heat to low and simmer, covered for 30 minutes until the corn tortillas have melted. Stir well and serve with a dollop of sour cream.

The corn tortillas create a wonderful flavor in this soup.

INDEX

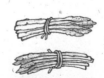

Blueberry

6 tablespoons softened butter
2/3 cup granulated sugar
2 eggs
1 teaspoon vanilla extract
2 teaspoons baking powder
1/4 teaspoon salt
2 cups sifted all-purpose flour
1/2 cup milk
2 cups fresh or frozen blueberries

Streusel topping:
2 tablespoons butter
2 tablespoons brown sugar
1/4 teaspoon cinnamon
1/2 cup chopped walnuts

Directions:

Heat oven to 375°. In a large bowl, cream together the butter and sugar until fluffy. Beat in the eggs. Add the vanilla extract, baking powder, and salt. Mix in half of the flour and the milk alternately, mixing gently by hand. Then add the remaining flour and milk. Stir in the blueberries. Fill greased muffin tins or foil baking cups.

To make the streusel topping, cut the butter into small pieces and mix it with the brown sugar, cinnamon, and walnuts. Sprinkle the topping over batter. Bake 25-30 minutes until muffins are lightly browned. Makes one dozen muffins.

You have heard it said that "necessity is the mother of invention".
If Dot Vartan ever doubted this adage, she now knows it to be true.
After the closing of a local bake shop where
she grew to become dependent on her "daily bread",
Dot was driven into her own kitchen
to invent over 100 muffin recipes to satisfy her craving.
Now you can benefit from this energetic lady's labor as she shares some of her favorites,
ranging from the far-from-banal basics to the epitome of the exotic,
all gracefully illustrated by Shelly Reeves Smith.
Too beautiful to keep to yourself, we know you'll want to share this book "Among Friends

THE AMONG FRIENDS LIBRARY